Exploring Nonviolent Alternatives

D1158939

Exploring Nonviolent Alternatives

By

Gene Sharp

introduction by
David Riesman

An Extending Horizons Book

Contents

Preface

We have been the victims of distortions of history and of the nature of political power. Many people believe that nonviolent means are incapable of achieving the changes they desire or of defending their principles or society against threats. Contrary to what we have been taught, there is a vast history of nonviolent struggle, much of which has been moderately effective. This despite the fact that nonviolent struggle is an underdeveloped technique, mostly improvised freshly on each occasion, lacking any of the advantages of study, preparations, training, and the like; all of which military struggle has normally had.

In addition, the doctrine that power derives from gun barrels, bullets, and explosive capacity (one sufficiently inaccurate and crude so that not even Hitler subscribed fully to it) has blinded people to the fundamental principle of all political power: that all power, of all groups and all governments, derives from sources in the society, and the availability of these is determined by the degree of cooperation and obedience offered by the people. This doctrine, when implemented through nonviolent struggle, makes it possible for people to realize their political potential and to struggle to control their own destinies, even against ruthless enemies well equipped with the machinery of violence.

For effective application, nonviolent struggle has requirements, as does violence; if these are not met it can fail, as can any other type of struggle. People differ in their estimates of the extent to which nonviolent action is, or can be made, sufficiently effective in actual combat to replace violence as the ultimate sanction and means of struggle. This question cannot be answered by dogmas, sermons, or niceties. There is need for vast study and research to provide the answer.

Although nonviolent action has been applied throughout history, in many cultures, civilizations, political systems, and conflict situations, although it has overthrown tyrants, defeated Nazis, immobilized armies, and brought power to the poor and the oppressed, it has never been explored seriously as a possible full replacement for violence. Why? It would be important to know. But it is still more important to correct this neglect, and to begin now deliberate explorations of the nature and potential of this nonviolent technique.

Introduction

by Professor David Riesman, Harvard University

For a good many years now, Mr. Sharp has been studying the uses of nonviolent action. He has examined not only the famous tactics and philosophy of Gandhi, but many instances where nonviolent resistance has been used by colonized people, by occupied people (as under the Nazis), and by factory workers. The present book is a continuation of such investigations, and includes essays on aspects of nonviolent resistance as well as a large bibliography. It should be useful in college courses, and for work with groups and individuals outside the universities engaged in exploring this terrain.

It is my impression that in the universities this is not a fashionable topic at the moment. Among one faction of the young and their adult acolytes, the fascination with violence is intense. Compared to the self-restraint of nonviolence, violence has the apparent advantage of seeming expressive. But the cult of expressivity is a fashion that defines what is to be expressed, and when spontaneity and impulsiveness become the valued qualities, they can be easily faked. Furthermore, there is a widespread view — held reluctantly by some, cheerfully by others – that "violence works." A high selectivity is often used to support this judgment. However, for the society as a whole the returns are not all in. Violent blacks, for instance, may have gained momentary tribute in a particular university or city, while helping elect Ronald Reagan to the Governorship or achieving some other larger negative outcome in state and nation. Similarly, radical white students may force a university to close down temporarily, and may in some cases even regard Ronald Reagan's victory to their advantage, but the battle is still going on and they have not seen the end of it. And in terms of therapeutic results for the violence-prone, the John Waynes of the Far Left, here also the returns are not all in. Once violence becomes an addiction, the personality changes; other more generous impulses are repressed; people become brutalized and declare that the society has made them that way.

There are situations in which a minority may be crushed whether or not it resists and however it resists. But nonviolent action requires great discipline and coherence, and thus reduces the negative side effects that violence produces quite apart from the physical casualties it inflicts. Because of the American bent for anarchic and impulsive violence, it is especially important to re-run some familiar historical scenarios with the nonviolent alternative in mind. To take first what may seem to be an outlandish example, can one imagine an American reaction to the attack on Pearl Harbor which would have declared that we would defend American territory, but would not carry an offensive war to the Japanese home islands? Instead we reacted with an almost instinctive eagerness for reprisal and an outburst of xenophobia. Or consider as another historical example the fondness a number of black militants (and their white supporters) have developed for the movie *The Battle of Algiers.* This semi-documentary is taken by them as suggesting a strategy for urban guerrilla warfare in the American city. Yet today some Algerians will say that the hatreds produced by this sort of warfare in which one escalated cruelty and intimidated one's own countrymen failed to prepare Algeria for the post-colonial situation or indeed misprepared it. A longer, slower, and perhaps equally risky policy of nonviolent action might have brought into being a better Algeria. The indiscriminate terror led to enormous casualties among Algerians and did nothing to heal the factionalism of the Algerian nationalist and radical movements down to the present time. And, as many have pointed out, Algeria was dealing with a foreign imperial power of another tongue and color, a distinct minority which could be driven out — while it is hard to imagine American urban blacks driving out the whites from their control over the resources necessary for the improvement of inner-city ghettos.[1]

A decade ago during the debate on civil defense against nuclear attack I was helping edit a journal called *The Correspondent* dealing with foreign affairs and strategic questions from what was then a minority point of view; we discussed questions of nonviolent defense as a form of active defense, in contrast to the offensive implications of the civil defense push which, had it succeeded, would have looked as if we were planning to attack the Soviet Union. We thought that a nation in a Hobbesian world needed some kind of defense and that it was politically impossible to persuade people otherwise. Today, the turn against nationalism by many newly radicalized Americans in the wake of the Vietnam war seems to have ended that kind of discussion of defense: many Americans are persuaded that the problem lies only inside America, in our own bellicosity and imperialism. Thus what matters is to assure our

1. Walter Metzger makes a useful distinction between strategies of de-exploitation and de-victimization among American blacks in "The Crisis of Academic Authority," *Daedalus,* Summer, 1970, Vol. 99, pp. 568-608.

defeat in Vietnam, and no further problems of American strategy will present themselves. If life were only so simple! Nationalism remains the strongest secular religion in the contemporary world, however we may regret the ethnocentrism and bellicosity that often accompany it. And paradoxically, some love of one's own country, one's own turf, seems to me essential for serious consideration of nonviolent strategies. One needs to take risks on behalf of one's country if one is not to surrender either to its own militarists or to those of other powers. Indeed, the militarists in one country are the allies of the militarists in another, against the interests of their own peoples in any case when they can manage to escalate an arms race. But in similar fashion, those who are interested in nonviolent alternatives are the allies of each other across national boundaries, just as Martin Luther King, Jr., could seek to put into practice in Mississippi what Gandhi had learned in Ahmedabad.

I believe it is easier to love a small country, and in some ways it may paradoxically be easier to defend one; the Danes under the Nazis are an illustration. Small nations can use nonviolent resistance to minimize the dangers of occupation or even "liberation." Large countries like our own that have nuclear weapons have discovered these to be lightning rods which actually reduce security and lead to heightened anxiety – Mr. Sharp also believes this. Such nations need to explore nonviolent alternatives as a method of beginning to dismantle the apparatus of weapons of mass destruction vis-à-vis their potential adversaries (perhaps maintaining a minimum nuclear deterrent in a stable underwater position as a kind of insurance until nonviolent action has gone further and people feel more confidence in it). Thus, both military men who love their country yet fear for it, and anti-militarists who are not wholly alienated from it, could well cooperate in strategic discussions of the possibilities and procedures of nonviolent defense.

Mr. Sharp's book is an appetizer in this direction, and is not intended as a full meal. He outlines many research areas that need investigation; but he does not himself touch directly on the degree to which the social character of important groups or of a whole nation facilitates or makes difficult developing the self-respect and mutual trust that nonviolent activism demands. Nor does he treat the problem of American masculinity which makes American men (with differing styles across the political and cultural spectrum) fearful to show fear and, at times, to remain nonviolent. We know little about the role of American women from different ethnic and social class backgrounds in taunting or tempting American men toward or away from violence. (Mr. Sharp uses *karate* and *jiu-jitsu* as metaphors for nonviolent defense against stronger force — metaphors which some versions of the women's liberation movement have taken as more than symbolic or suggestive.) The subtle dialectic among Americans between team spirit and anarchic impulse seems to me to make the discipline of nonviolent defense extremely difficult, although in this area experiments in training by American Friends Service Committee groups and the periodically successful use of marshals in peace demonstrations help keep alive the possibilities of further development.

Yet fully to pursue those possibilities requires a diminution of impatience: a willingness even in the midst of crisis to avoid hysterical reactions born of despair or the cult of expressivity. Impatience interferes with curiosity about alternatives, and often rests on the premise that our society is overwhelmingly rotten and repressive and that there is nothing further to be learned about it.

Most of the young people who argue this way have had, of course, no direct experience with totalitarian societies. Their fear of an over-controlled society may be as much the outcome of their actual experience of permissiveness as of haphazard encounters, for example, with our frequently *xiii* wayward but rarely systematic police. Perhaps they have also inherited the continuing American tendency to over-estimate the power of totalitarian societies; I argued in 1951 that we were fascinated and awed by such societies and failed to see the degree to which they were permeable and incompetent: they could kill people but not always control them.[2] In any event, most Americans find the talk about repression on the part of university radicals and black militants incomprehensible, in the face of evidences everywhere that the counter-culture flourishes. Neverthe-less, a Right-wing *coup* is conceivable in the United States, though I regard it as perhaps somewhat less likely than a further breakdown of social control and a further disinte-gration of social bonds. Whatever the chances, studies of nonviolent alternatives provide insurance against domestic as against foreign mischance – the same kind of insur-ance that armies and weaponry diminishingly provide. The provision of armies and weapons damages domestic society by diverting human talents and material resources. In contrast, work and research and experiment on the science and art of nonviolent alternatives, it seems to me, can only benefit society by turning attention to ourselves and our relations with each other as the main resource, the main insurance for survival.

2. See Riesman, "Some Observations on the Limits of Totalitarian Power," reprinted in *Abundance for What?* (Doubleday, 1963), pp. 80-92, and dis-cussion on pp. 6-8.

1

Creative Conflict in Politics

In facing the problem of conflict today in national and international politics, we are confronted by an apparent dilemma. Both the waging and the failure to wage such conflict may lead to disastrous consequences.

Consider a few of the symbols of modern political conflict: Vietnam, Cambodia, Czechoslovakia, Jackson State, Kent State, the Middle East, the assassinations of the Kennedys and King, Watts, Newark, Greece, Northern Ireland — and what will it be tomorrow? Only a few years ago such symbols were Spain, Algeria, Hungary, Angola, Belsen, Dresden, Hiroshima. These cases point both to the severe dangers of modern methods of political struggle and to the urgent need for effective means of conducting political conflicts.

In many such cases, real issues are at stake, and the outcome of such struggles will help to determine what kind of a future, if any, humanity will have. They are issues on which a struggle is worthwhile. The dilemma enters when both submission and struggle lead to tragedy. *1*

How, then, can one speak seriously of "creative conflict in politics"?

This one certainly cannot do if one argues for the total adequacy of the traditional answers to the problem of political conflict. Many of these are nobly motivated. Many are highly useful within particular types of situations. Many have made useful contributions in the past and still have a role to play in the future. But the fact must be faced that these means of dealing with political conflicts do not contain a sufficient answer to the problem now facing us.

Let us consider a few of these briefly. The admitted merits of some of them are too well known to require repetition here. We are concerned with the reasons why, such merits accepted, these are in present conditions insufficient.

1. Removal of causes: While in the long run this will help, we are left with present conflicts and future ones which develop despite such efforts. Further, where real issues are at stake, knowledge of the origin of the conflict does not remove it, nor does such knowledge prevent resort to means of struggle which are themselves tragic.

2. Increased understanding of the opponent: This is an important contribution, but is no self-evident solution to our problem. Understanding may not remove the issues at stake, nor does it affect the power relationships. In some cases, fuller understanding of the opponent's ideology and intentions may even heighten the conflict.

3. Compromise: This is very useful in many types of situations where no serious matter of principle or question concerning the basic direction or purpose of the society is at stake. Where, however, such matters are involved, there exist issues on which compromise is both morally and politically dangerous. In such cases, some form of violent conflict has usually been the means of last resort.

4. Negotiation, conciliation, arbitration: These are important aspects of the resolution of many conflicts.

These methods often involve compromise, and its strengths and weaknesses therefore apply here as well. In addition, there is the question of what means of struggle or sanction is held in the background of such procedures to which resort may be had if acceptable results are not thus achieved.

5. *Democratic institutions:* While acknowledging their contribution, they are not totally adequate, for (a) they do not exist everywhere; (b) nominally democratic countries have practiced undemocratic and inhuman deeds; (c) the internal power structure of such a society may impose a *de facto* limitation on a democratic government's responsiveness to popular control; and (d) there is no established means in a parliamentary system to deal with extensive internal subversion, guerrilla warfare, violent rebellion, *coup d'état* and military invasion, without resort to violent conflict.

6. *World government:* While not denying the value of international agencies and institutions, to suggest that the major solution to the present problem of international, or even intra-national, conflict lies here is to ignore: (a) the small likelihood of such a super-State being established as long as major international conflicts and the power struggle continue; (b) the dangers to freedom involved in concentrating sufficient power in a world political unit to be able to suppress conflicts throughout the world; and (c) the absence of a peaceful method of dealing with a "world civil war" under such a system.

7. *Violent revolution:* In conflicts with oppressors, the traditional means of last resort has been violent revolution. Apart from the question of its long-term results, this response suffers from two limitations: (a) the chances of victory are now reduced in proportion to the degree that the revolutionaries depend for success upon military means and to the degree that the opponent is a modern State in whose hands superior military resources are concentrated; and (b) the possibility of foreign military aid to counter

3

this situation is reduced or made highly dangerous by the present risks of the spread of war, especially where a protagonist in the world power struggle is involved.

8. War: Whatever may have been true previously, a major war can no longer be used as a rational means of conducting or resolving conflicts. Even the theory of deterrence involves severe dangers, and is *at best,* taking claims for granted, a means of gaining time for the intervention of other means.

9. Avoidance of provocation: The plea that the sole cause of external military threats lies in provocative military preparations ignores other causes of aggressive military action and instances of it where no provocation existed.

10. Apathy and impotence: As problems appear vast, and the chances of the individual being able to do anything effective about them appear small, the attitude spreads that there is no use in even trying. This contributes to increasing apathy toward major issues and conflicts, assisting the development of increasingly subtle means of social control, ending perhaps in some new form of tyranny.

One reason why some of these responses to conflict are not sufficient and others are undesirable is that they do not fulfil the same function as that fulfilled by various forms of violent conflict. In the past, if no acceptable settlement of a conflict was forthcoming by negotiation, etc., one always had an alternative to passive submission to the opponent's claims. One could resort to violence as an ultimate sanction, as a means of struggle, in the hope of later achieving an acceptable settlement.

Many of the results of such violence were undesirable. Morally, it left a bad taste with many people. In many wars, furthermore, no humanitarian issue or question of principle was really at stake and they could without any loss to humanity have never been fought.

4   But where significant issues of principle have been at

stake, violent conflict has relieved people of a sense of impotence, and provided a means – however unsatisfactory – by which they could struggle for their convictions and objectives. Violence has in such cases seemed justifiable to most people. Passivity and acquiescence when "talking" had failed was unacceptable to them, both morally and politically.

Yet none of the other listed means of dealing with conflicts offers a substitute means of action to fulfil the same function. This is undoubtedly one of the most important reasons why so many people have reluctantly accepted the continued need for various forms of violent conflict.

If the apparent trend towards authoritarianism and totalitarianism in many countries and under several political systems is not effectively challenged and reversed, an extension of autocratic social and political organization is likely.

With the developments in military power and modern weapons, the ultimate means of action – violent conflict – has in such crises, for reasonable men, been removed at a point of great need for effective means of struggle. We are thus faced with an apparent dilemma: there is grave danger in the failure to conduct such conflicts; however, there is even greater danger in conducting them by the accepted means. People unwilling to submit may nevertheless resort to violent revolution or war. Or, knowing no way out, people may slide increasingly into apathy and escapism.

An important problem thus remains without an answer: how to conduct such conflicts without producing disaster by the methods used. Where the basic issues admit no compromise, what ultimate sanction can be relied upon which is at least as effective as other possible means, but does not in its consequences destroy the principles and humanity on whose behalf the struggle was launched?

Are there creative means of struggle and sanctions which 5

can be applied where we have previously relied upon violence? Are there means of struggle which deal effectively with the conflict and also contribute to the growth of a more humane social order?

Our answer to the tragedy of modern political conflict must accept conflict as an inevitable part of human society. To the degree that our answer provides a creative means of facing, conducting and resolving such conflicts, it may help the society to develop greater inner consistency and integration.

We need a technique of conducting conflicts, which is effective and capable of coping with the reality of power, while dealing with the situation creatively and contributing to the development of social relationships and a social order compatible with humanitarian ideals.

There has been some experience with a technique which appears to have a sufficient degree of such qualities to merit further investigation. Let us, therefore, sketch very briefly the events in several cases where it has been applied.

The Norwegian Sports Strike

During the Nazi occupation of Norway, Norwegians repeatedly refused to cooperate politically either with Germans or with the Norwegian fascist party, the *Nasjonal Samling*. One of the lesser known parts of this resistance is the Norwegian sports strike.

In the summer of 1940, local German officers sought local football teams to play teams of German soldiers. At first such matches took place, but they were soon halted on the basis of a policy adopted by both national Norwegian sports organizations in the autumn of 1939 ordering their branches not to play with foreign teams. (This had been intended as support for Norwegian neutrality amidst a tense Europe already at war, but the pre-invasion policy was soon seen to work as a means of declining German overtures.)[1] Germans then tried to join

Norwegian sports clubs. Officers especially sought out tennis clubs. The Norwegians succeeded in declining such an influx of unwanted members. Where German pressure was most persistent, it was settled that the Germans might requisition or rent the tennis courts one or two days a week; the club members then stayed completely away those days, refusing to play with the invaders and thwarting those attempts by the Nazis to build friendships with the Norwegians.[2]

Early in September of 1940 the two sports organizations united into Norway's Sports Association, with no influence from the political situation or the new government. However, on September 25, a "commissar-ish Minister" for work service and sports was named, Alex Stang (whose interest in sports had hitherto been unknown to the sports world). The chairman of the new Norway's Sports Association, Olaf Helset, met with Stang twice and twice by telephone had made it clear that there must be no interference in the self-government and independence of the sports organization. On September 22 the new united sports organization had rejected a proposal that international sports contests be arranged with neighboring countries. On October 1, Stang, in a radio talk, urged all sports youth to gather in the new association, and next day he issued instructions to that association: "The prohibition against international cooperation is lifted as of today."[3] Further attempts to regulate the activities of the sports organization followed. Finally, the steering committee of Norway's Sports Association sent to the branches over the country a circular letter of orientation on the fascist efforts thus far to establish party control over the sports organization (a copy of which found its way to Axel Stang, together with a covering letter stating that should the Department hold fast to the line it had set, the steering committee would be unable to continue). The circular letter indicated that the committee considered itself in no position to continue its activities, and the 7 specifics of dealing with the situation were left to the members. No instructions or recommended lines of action were given.

On November 22, Stang announced the establishment of Norway's Sports Association, with its constitution set by his Department; the dissolution of constituent organizations was prohibited without Departmental permission. Further, "leaders" would be named for each sports organization; there would be no more elected chairmen or committees.

With one exception, all named sports officials resolved they could not cooperate with the New Order in sports. A protest letter was drafted, sent to Stang, and later distributed in circulars and illegal newspapers. The letter ended with a warning that the State action was injurious to Norwegian sports, and exceeded the law. Sports officials surrendered the keys and archives of the organizations to the Department, and stated that legal, moral, and economic responsibility now lay with the State Minister.

It was clear that initiative for further action lay with the members of the various sports groups throughout the country. The first occasion for action came almost immediately.

Plans for wrestling matches between Norway and Denmark had been laid almost as soon as the prohibition against international contests had been declared lifted. When the fascist sports official arrived in Tönsberg, where the matches were to be held, he was told that the 64 Norwegian wrestlers who were to participate had all stayed away. Olaf Helset, who had been chairman of Norway's Sports Association before N.S. control, wrote: "And thereby the sports front was really created. Now it was clear that the active sports youths would have nothing to do with the New Order. Now it was necessary to hold the front."[4]

With few exceptions, all the activities of the fascist-controlled sports organizations were boycotted throughout the occupation; this included both participation in and attendance at official sports events and contests. (Illegal and unofficial sports contests were held and were highly attended; official matches attracted almost no spectators.)

Helset later described the strike as ". . . the unconditional *no* to every demand for participation in sports contests in which Germans were present, and to the edict to be part of the sports movement for the 'New Order' . . . . And its moral significance for the whole resistance movement lay both in that it was the first organized rally against the German administrative attack and in that it continued under all pressures as long as the war lasted."[5]

The sports strike was not simply conducted on the basis of orders from above, but rather arose from underneath the leaders and within the sports groups throughout the country. Thomas Wyller, a political scientist analyzing the resistance of these years, points out that the resistance of the sportsmen "became an example which showed the way when other organizations later were confronted with the choice between existing in a new form or to lay down their activities.[6]

An eminent historian of the period, Magne Skodvin, writes:

The sports strike extended over the whole country and gathered the greater part of the youth. When the sports people disappeared from the sports grounds — and from the newspaper columns, when they stopped appearing officially completely, then one had either to be very stupid or very much like a hermit not to notice it. The Germans and N.S. suffered a serious defeat when the sportsmen refused to play, and no tolerably awake Norwegian could be blind to the patterns which were thereby given.[7]

This pattern of noncooperation was followed by other occupational groups, as the teachers, and blocked the establishment of the fascist Corporate State in Norway.

The sports strike was not officially broken until June 3, 1945, when parades of thousands of sportsmen and crowds of people on occasions all over Norway celebrated the end of the struggle and the initiation of new, free sports activities.

India

At the end of the 1920s, advocates of violent revolution had gained an impressive following and bombs were not infrequently thrown. However, the Indian National Congress accepted Gandhi's leadership in formulating a nonviolent campaign for self-government.[8]

For the 1930 campaign, Gandhi chose nonviolent noncooperation and civil disobediance. He formulated a program of political demands, and a plan for nonviolent rebellion. Pleas to the Viceroy failed to produce concessions.

Focusing initially on the Salt Act (which imposed a heavy tax and a Government monopoly), Gandhi set out with disciples on a 26-day march to the sea to commit civil disobedience by making salt. After weighing the *pros* and *cons* the Government waited until later to arrest him.

The making of salt by Gandhi was the signal for mass nonviolent revolt throughout the country. As the movement progressed, there were mass meetings, huge parades, making of seditious speeches, boycott of foreign cloth and picketing of liquor shops and opium dens. Students left government schools. The national flag was hoisted. There were social boycotts on government employees, short strikes *(hartals),* and resignations by government employees and Members of the Legislative Assembly and Councils.

Government departments were boycotted, as were foreign insurance firms, postal and telegraph services. Many refused to pay taxes. Some renounced titles. There were nonviolent raids and seizures of government-held salt.

The Government arrested Gandhi early in the campaign. *10* About 100,000 Indians (including 17,000 women) were imprisoned or held in detention camps. There were beatings, injuries, censorship, shootings, confiscation, intimidation, fines, banning of meetings, and organizations, and other measures. Some were shot dead.

During the year, the normal functioning of government was severely affected and great suffering experienced by the resisters. A truce was finally agreed, under terms settled by direct negotiations between Gandhi and the Viceroy.

Although concessions were made to the nationalists, the actual terms favored the government more than the nationalists. More important, however, in Gandhi's view was that the strength thus generated in the Indians meant that independence could not long be denied, and the fact that by having to participate in direct negotiations with the nonviolent rebels the Government had recognized India as an equal, with whose representatives she had to negotiate. This was as upsetting to Churchill as it was reassuring to Gandhi.

In Vykom,[9] Travancore, South India, untouchables had for centuries been forbidden to use a particular road leading directly to their quarters because the road passed an orthodox Brahmin temple. After consultations with Gandhi, in 1924, high caste Hindus initiated action.

A group of themselves and untouchable friends walked down the road, stopping in front of the temple. The orthodox Hindus attacked them severely, and some were arrested, receiving prison sentences of up to a year.

Volunteers poured in from all parts of India, and instead of further arrests, the Maharajah's government ordered police to prevent the reformers from entering the road. A cordon was placed across it. The reformers stood in an attitude of prayer before it, pleading with the police to allow them to pass. Both groups organized day and night shifts. The reformers pledged themselves to nonviolence. They refused to withdraw until the Brahmins recognized *11* the right of the untouchables to use the highway. As the months passed, the numbers of the reformers and their spirits sometimes rose and sometimes fell.

When the rainy season came and the road was flooded, they stood by their posts, shortening their shifts to three hours as the water reached their shoulders. Police kept the cordon in boats.

When the Government finally removed the barrier, the reformers declined to walk forward until the orthodox Hindus had changed their attitude. After sixteen months the Brahmins said: "We cannot any longer resist the prayers that have been made to us, and we are ready to receive the untouchables."

The case had widespread reverberations throughout India, assisting in the removal of similar restrictions elsewhere and in strengthening the cause of caste reform.

El Salvador

In late April and early May 1944, one of the most ruthless of the Latin American dictators found his mighty power dissolved by a massive nonviolent civilian insurrection. The *Inter-American* reported at the time:[10]

> After thirteen bloody years, General Maximiliano Hernández Martínez was forced out of the Presidency of El Salvador on May 9 by a force which he hardly believed existed: the will of the people.
>
> It seemed that the only will which *salvadoreños* knew was that of their master. Occasionally a few troublemakers stirred up a little discontent here and there. But it never grew serious, for the machine-guns took care of it nicely.
>
> After the [violent] revolt of early April had been crushed, Hernández started his usual man-hunt. Anyone suspected of even the remotest connection with the revolt was hunted down and shot or jailed. Many were tortured in an effort to get the names of others.

All newspapers except Hernández' mouthpiece, *Diario Nuevo,* were closed.

Everything was calm, said the official reports. Fifty-three had been killed in the revolution, and another score had been executed for complicity. But the reports brought out by refugees counted the executed in the thousands, and the imprisoned in still more thousands.

Colonel Tito Calvo, actual leader of the attempt, was dead. Dr. Arturo Romero, beloved San Salvador teacher, believed to have encouraged Calvo, was in jail, wounded and under sentence of death.

On April 24, the country's students printed and distributed a leaflet which called for a general strike and gave specific directions.

This leaflet, reported by *Newsweek,*[11] was titled: "Decree for a general strike including hospitals, courts, and public works." Part of the text read:

The basis of the strike shall be general passive resistance, noncooperation with the government, the wearing of mourning, the unity of all classes, the prohibition of fiestas.

By showing the tyrant the abyss between him and the people, by isolating him completely, we shall cause his downfall. Boycott the movies, the newspapers, the national lottery. Pay no taxes. Abandon government jobs. Leave them unfilled. Pray daily for the souls of the massacred. The Archbishop has been humiliated.

The recommendations were followed, the *Inter-American* account continues:

Acting on their own instructions, high school and university students walked out. Within a week the   *13* country was paralyzed. Postal and government offices were vacant, stores were closed, garbage piled up in the streets; trains, streetcars, and busses stopped running. Hospitals were deserted by doctors, and the courts by lawyers and judges. Women wore mourning in the streets, and by May 6, the banks and factories shut down.

The bewildered Hernández, whose practice was to tell his Ministers what to do, now asked for their advice. Resign, said the Cabinet. Meekly, the President resigned, and the Constituent Assembly appointed the stocky, sixty-two-year-old Minister of Defense, General Andrés I. Menéndez to the Presidency *pro tem.* General Menéndez is not thought to be a front man for Hernández, and is expected to call a general election soon. He allowed the press to resume operation and ordered amnesty for all political refugees.

Only after their erstwhile dictator had left for Guatemala would *salvadoreños* go back to work. Few men have seen their permanent departure hailed with such joy.

In Guatemala City, Hernández said he would become a farmer. "I bear no ill will to anyone," he said forgivingly.

Shortly, the contagion had spread, and Guatemala's dictator, Martinez, fell in face of resistance patterned on the El Salvadorean pattern.[12]

Russia

Among the 250,000 political prisoners in the coal-mining camps at Vorkuta,[13] strikes against poor conditions had long been considered. The decision was precipitated just after Stalin's death in 1953 by the announcement by the MVD (the secret police) there that political
14 prisoners ought not to expect an amnesty, since their

liberation would jeopardize the security of the State.

Many waverers then cast their lot with those advocating nonviolent resistance; by the end of May, strike committees were secretly established in several camps. They were composed of three groups of prisoners: Leninist students, anarchists, and the *Monashki* (a post-revolutionary pacifist Christian group resembling the early Quakers), plus prisoners representing no group.

Beria's fall encouraged more waverers. Strike committees were set up in the coal mining pits where they worked. The strike was to demand abolition of the camps and change of the prisoners' status to that of free colonists under contract. When, before the strike began, the central leadership was arrested and removed to Moscow, a new committee was elected.

On July 21 many prisoners remained in their barracks, refusing to work. They insisted on presenting their demands only to the commandant of all the Vorkuta camps, which they did two days later when 30,000 had joined the strike. Then the General made a long speech containing vague promises and specific threats.

A week passed without decisive action; no clear orders came from Moscow. Food would continue only while existing provisions lasted, it was announced. A strike leaflet appeared in thousands of copies urging self-reliance to gain freedom, and the strike as the only possible means of action. Sympathetic soldiers helped to spread these and to maintain contacts between the camps. Twenty big pits were shut down.

Russian-speaking troops were then withdrawn and replaced by soldiers from the Far East tribes. With the strike at its peak in early August, the State Prosecutor arrived with several generals from Moscow, offering minor concessions: two letters home a month (instead of a year), one visit a year, removal of identification numbers from clothes and of iron bars from barracks windows.

In an open letter, the strike leadership rejected these. *15*

The Prosecutor spoke at the camps, promising better food, higher pay, shorter shifts. Only a few wavered. The Strike Committee leaders went to an interview with the General, but never returned.

After holding out for over three months the strike finally ended in face of food and fuel shortages. Considerable material improvements were made, and a spokesman of the International Commission on Concentration Camp Practices considered the strike action in this and other camps to have been one of the most important factors in the improvement in the lot of the political prisoners.

America

On December 1, 1955, in Montgomery, Alabama, a tired Negro seamstress, along with three others, was asked, in accordance with local practice, to give up her bus seat to a newly-boarded white man, and stand.[14] Three complied, but Mrs. Parks, having had enough of such treatment, refused.

A one-day protest against her arrest by boycotting the buses on December 5th was nearly 100 per cent effective. It was decided to continue the boycott indefinitely until major reforms in the policy were made. Evening mass meetings in churches overflowed. The response, in both numbers and spirit, exceeded all hopes.

Negroes walked, took taxis and shared rides, but stayed off the buses. A new spirit of dignity and self-respect permeated the Negro community. The whites were confronted by qualities they had not believed the Negroes possessed.

The aim became improvement of the whole community. The appeal was to Christian love. The young Rev. Martin Luther King, Jr., and his co-workers, found themselves thrust into leadership and international prominence.

Negotiations failed to produce a satisfactory settlement. The use of taxis at reduced fares was prohibited. A car pool of 300 vehicles was organized. Money began to pour in, and a fleet of over 15 new station wagons was added. Many Negroes preferred to walk as a concrete expression of their determination and dedication. They grew in awareness of the nature of nonviolent action and love in conflict.

False rumors were spread about the movement's leaders, along with false reports of a settlement. Negro drivers were arrested for minor, often imaginary, traffic violations. Police intimidation became common.

Rev. King was arrested on a charge of speeding. Over thirty threatening phone calls and letters reached the leaders daily, often signed "KKK." King's home was bombed; Negroes nearly broke into violence, but calm was restored. Another home was bombed. Nearly 100 Negro leaders were arrested, charged with violating an anti-boycott law.

Fear, long known by Southern Negroes, was cast off. Many went to the sheriff's office, hoping to be among those "wanted." The trial — receiving world attention — became a testimony of fearlessness and a recounting of grievances. The movement gained new momentum.

A suit was filed by the Negroes in the Federal District Court, which declared the city bus segregation laws unconstitutional. The city appealed to the U.S. Supreme Court.

Meanwhile the bus protest continued, asking now an end to bus segregation. Insurance policies on the station wagons were cancelled; they were transferred to a London firm. City officials declared the car pool illegal. The same day the U.S. Supreme Court affirmed the unconstitutionality of the bus segregation laws.

That night the mass meeting emphasized love, dignity and refusal to ride the buses until segregation was abolished. Also, that night the Ku Klux Klan rode through the Negro district. Instead of locked dark houses of terrified Negroes, the lights were on, the doors open, and people watched the Klan parade, a few even waving. *17*

Nonplussed, the Klan disappeared.

With the car pool prohibited, each area worked out its own share-the-ride plan, and many walked. The buses remained empty. In the mass meetings, detailed plans were presented for resuming – after over a year – the use of the buses on an integrated basis. There must be no boasting of rights, no pushing, but courtesy, it was insisted. This was a victory, not over the white man, but for justice and democracy.

The Court's bus integration order finally reached Montgomery on December 20th. On the first day of integration, there were no major incidents.

Then the white extremists began a reign of terror. Shots were fired at buses. A teenage girl was beaten. A pregnant Negro woman was shot in the leg. The Klan paraded again. But the Negroes' fear of them had gone. A small Negro boy warmed his hands at one of the burning crosses.

Then the homes of more leaders and several Negro churches were bombed. This turned the tide against the white supremacists. The local newspaper, several white ministers and the businessmen's association denounced the bombings.

The Negroes adhered to nonviolence. More bombs exploded. Arrested whites were quickly found not guilty, but the disturbances abruptly ceased. The desegregation proceeded smoothly, and in a few weeks transport was back to normal, with Negroes and whites sitting where they pleased on integrated buses – a compliance with the court order that would have been virtually inconceivable, without the forces set in operation by the Negroes' nonviolent action.

Cuba

The Cuban revolution against Fulgencio Batista is best known for its bands of guerrillas in the mountains of the Sierra Madre and its ideologs of guerrilla warfare.[15] A significant number of nonviolent action methods were, however, applied to undermine the Batista dictatorship, including marches, nonviolent protests and strikes. There were three general strikes during the revolution, the third of which was called by Fidel Castro as the climax of the struggle to ensure that no *coup d'état* should steal his revolution in its final hours.

The first island-wide general strike began on July 30, 1957. Following the funeral of the murdered Frank Païs, leader of urban resistance, students spontaneously ran through the streets of Santiago crying "Strike!" The independent civic resistance had long wished to call a general strike but did not know how to organize one in the situation. By morning of August 1 the city, Cuba's second largest, was paralyzed. The strike spread, reaching Havana by August 5. Police terror had already begun, however, and the strike received no backing from either the government-controlled union, the C.T.C., nor from the Communist-controlled union. When workers in Havana returned to work before hardly beginning, disheartened Santiago workers capitulated on August 6, having produced five and a half days of economic paralysis in Santiago. Batista thought he had won, and the *Resistencia Cívica* thought they had failed. But it was more complicated. There had been no planning, no alternate distribution of food, and no means to counter police invasions of homes in Havana. However, in addition to the economic paralysis, in the cities of eastern Cuba the population became sufficiently radicalized so that police never again conducted counter-revolutionary terror, as they had done in December 1955 and January 1956. Santiago became a stronghold of revolutionary fervor which the Batista government could never count on ruling.

The urban section of the 26th of July Movement was heartened by the possibilities shown by this method. Consequently they presented to Castro a plan for a general strike to be called in the spring of 1958. Castro opposed the particular plan, since it called for the strike to be *19* planned in secret, for strike action at different times in different places, and for enforcement by armed guerrillas in the streets. Ché Guevara wrote: "... their conception of a general strike was too narrow." The strike failed. In Santiago, an early event of the day had been an armed rising of about two hundred untrained urban fighters. Ché Guevara wrote: "... the National Committee of the Movement, having blundered utterly concerning the rudiments of mass struggle, had attempted to start the strike by surprise, with no advance notice – with shooting."[16] The strike was fairly effective in Oriente Province, but again not in Havana. The organizers had not even contacted student groups about the student strike plan, or workers about the labor strike. By evening in Havana the armed rebels were dead and the strike was over; Santiago lost heart, and the strike collapsed everywhere.

This failure was disastrous to the practice of nonviolent resistance in the revolution and to the urban movement all over Cuba. There were no more demonstrations or militant nonviolent demonstrations to Batista. The people just waited. Castro angrily blamed the urban leaders, arguing that such extreme secrecy in planning was not good in a nonviolent program.[17] Most of the 26th of July forces were withdrawn from the cities, and the people's confidence in nonviolent methods was shaken. However, Batista never again returned to his drastic repressive measures in the cities.

It was late autumn 1958 before Castro was again able to consider calling the climactic general strike; by then his forces had cut the country in half and controlled Oriente. He felt that if an effective general strike were called, it would win the revolution without the bloodshed that would be required for his military forces to conquer the island. He expected this general strike to be "... the final stroke..." Before this strike could be planned, however, Batista fled the country, on January 1, 1959. Fearing a coup to step into the power vacuum, Castro went on Rebel

Radio and appealed to the workers for a general strike to prevent such a take-over. There had been some rioting in Havana, and General Cantillo had threatened to seize the government. After Castro's appeal for a strike, however, the people became peaceful and concentrated on making the general strike a success. U.S. Ambassador Smith wrote: "... with ... the revolutionaries in control, the general strike was completely effective."[18] The sequence might have been reversed. The revolution, therefore, ended nonviolently with a minimum of immediate terror in reprisals which had marked earlier changes of government in Cuba. Castro clearly recognized the important role which nonviolent resistance had played in the revolution and was committed to its revolutionary potential to the end. It was to this which he turned to prevent the victory being seized by a military take-over, while his military forces were still days of fighting away from Havana. True power, it seemed, came not from the barrels of his guns, but from the power of a united people.

There are many other examples which might be cited of this type of movement: the Moslem "Servants of God" movement led by Khan Abdul Ghaffar Khan in the North-West Frontier Province of British India; the actions of Danilo Dolci in Sicily, the civil disobedience actions of the unilateralists in Britain, the Danish resistance to the Nazi occupation, Czechoslovakia in 1968, and many others in almost every part of the world.

This is the phenomenon of nonviolent action. It has been called by various names: passive resistance, Satyagraha, positive action, nonviolent resistance, nonviolent direct action.

Gandhi has been its modern prophet, and he made major improvements in the technique. He refined and consciously developed its strategy, tactics and methods. He combined mass political action with a moral rejection of violence. He coupled direct action with a constructive *21* program for social reconstruction.

Yet it cannot be dismissed as a "peculiarly Indian" or "Hindu" phenomenon. Its practice by Moslems, Christians, atheists and others in various parts of the world before, during and since Gandhi's time is evidence to the contrary.

Further, in various places under totalitarian rule, as in the examples of Norway and Vorkuta, the technique has been applied with no evidence of significant Gandhian influence.

In recent years, the practice has spread rapidly. It is, perhaps, not without significance that the emergence of this technique to prominence in the political arena has taken place in the same half-century as the emergence of the totalitarian State and nuclear war. On the one hand is power which relies on suppression and destruction. On the other, is power relying on noncooperation, intervention, and nonviolent moral courage.

Remarkable, too, is it that this technique, which is being used by people, often in the face of overwhelming obstacles, to assert their participation in determining their own destinies, has emerged to significance in an era of political manipulation and widespread feelings of impotence.

In the years of some of the most blatant crimes against humanity, a technique of action has expanded in the political arena which may be applied without violation of the actionists' moral values. Perhaps it is equally significant that it has provided a means of conducting important conflicts for humanitarian objectives, without the significant weaknesses of the traditional methods of action.

There are important indications that this type of action is a far more creative response to the conflict situation, and that it helps to create a more satisfactory resolution of the conflict and to build a better social order. As violence is closely associated with tyranny, injustice and war, the nonviolent nature of this response may have far-reaching 22 effects, associated with freedom, justice and peace.

There is the problem of the extent to which nonviolent action is suitable as a substitute for violent conflict and violent sanctions. We are concerned, it is recalled, not with applying this technique every time a disagreement appears, for there are many other ways of dealing with most conflicts, and solving them. It is a question of means of action in conflicts which are not resolved by the normal means, and of an ultimate sanction.

There has been enough experience with nonviolent action to establish that it cannot be flatly dismissed as a substitute for violence, at least on some occasions. The problem therefore becomes one of the extent to which this substitution is possible. Here opinions differ considerably, and our desire here is not to present dogmatic conclusions, but to suggest areas in which further thought, knowledge and experimentation might be useful in seeking an answer to our central problem.

We must keep in mind in this discussion the present limitations on violent conflict, the dangers of having no means of struggle, and the relatively limited state of our knowledge of nonviolent action. In some of these areas, the substitution has been largely already made. In others, it has only to a limited degree, while in still other situations, the idea seems improbable to most observers.

1. In labor disputes: Here the substitution of a few nonviolent methods, the strike and boycott, for violence was made long ago, and there are very few voices advocating a return to violence in such conflicts. The form of action has often been applied without a compatible spirit, and little attention has been given to other nonviolent forms which are available. (The form of struggle, i.e., whether it is violent or nonviolent, must not be assumed to be the same as whether basic or minor changes are made in institutions, ownership, and control. Nonviolent means can lead to either, depending on how they are used and what is desired.)

2. In minority group grievances: There has been a rapid   *23* growth in the substitution of nonviolent action for both violence and passivity among minorities feeling oppressed or discriminated against in recent years. The use of nonviolent action by the Southern Negroes, the civil disobedience of Tamils in Ceylon, and of South African Indians are examples of this. It is often clear that violence would be useless in such situations, while the conventional means of change are often inadequately available or inappropriate.

3. In peasant struggles: Nonviolent action has been used on a limited scale in such conflicts as the Bardoli satyagraha campaign of 1928 and in post-independence peasant movements in India and in South America. A major substitution has not taken place; however, the tendency of violence to bring severe repression and guerrila war to bring foreign involvement, may contribute to new developments in nonviolent land struggles.

4. In colonial liberation movements: Here there has been wide recognition of nonviolent action as a possible alternative to violence. In the remaining colonial struggles, the trend is now toward violence.

5. In issues of "no compromise": Where a group of the populace differs basically trom government policies on matters of principle on which no compromise is seen as possible, a traditional response has been violent rioting, political terrorism, and sometimes violent revolt. Nonviolent action has provided in Britain in the unilateral nuclear disarmament movement and in France among Frenchmen opposed to the Algerian War an alternative peaceful means of opposition. Similar actions have been used in the U.S. against the war in Indo-China.

6. In revolutions against tyrants: Still less consensus exists here, although it is significant that nonviolent struggle played a major part in the Dutch, Norwegian, and Danish resistance movements during World War II, the East German Revolt (1953) and (along with violence) in the

Hungarian Revolution. There is a widespread view that the political circumstances may be a determining factor in deciding which technique is suitable.

7. In national defense policies: There has been no case of a deliberate substitution of nonviolent action for military means as a national defense policy, although the Danish and Czechoslovak decisions to forego military resistance to invasion but to resist by other means after the occupation, and several cases of nonviolent action under occupations, are relevant. A defense policy of advance training of the populace in resistance by nonviolent methods as a means of meeting possible invasion and of deterring such invasion by making the chances of a successful occupation small, is now being actively proposed for investigation in some countries, among them Britain, Sweden, Denmark, Norway, Germany, Japan, Austria, and the United States. The present limits of war, and the reality of tyranny may make this a more reasonable possibility than may appear at first sight.

8. In meeting a coup d'état: The general strike in 1920 in Germany against the Kapp *Putsch* is probably the main experience thus far in the use of nonviolent action as the main sanction to defend the existing government against a *coup d'état*. In light of the difficulties of other possible courses where the army supports a *coup,* various methods of nonviolent action may merit consideration.

9. In providing domestic sanctions: The possibility of substituting nonviolent sanctions for violent ones (police, prisons, etc.) has scarcely been considered, although there have been small attempts in India to develop a nonviolent corps as a substitute for police in quelling riots, guarding villages from bandits, and so on.

Certain types of law on social policy, for example laws against child-labor or racial discrimination, might be enforced, after investigation and negotiation, not by imprisonment but by officially approved boycotts, non-cooperation, strikes, etc. against the offending firm. In an 25 age of increasing concentration of power in the State, such possibilities may not be entirely unreasonable.

The South African situation still provides a chance for the co-ordination of renewed and expanded nonviolent action by the internal resistance movement, as well as international action through such means as the economic boycott, refusal to cooperate with South African bodies except those practicing racial integration, political pressures at the United Nations, refusal to supply any sort of arms to the South African Government, and many other measures, undertaken on a mass scale.

Conflict there is, and sanctions there must be. But there is also the opportunity in this case of applying sanctions which, while wielding effective power in the situation, also allow for creativity and contribute to a positively better society in the future. It will be sad if this opportunity for combined action is lost. Gestures are insufficient. This could provide a pattern for dealing by such means with future tyrants.

All this has nothing to do with the question of "pacifism" as it has traditionally been posed. That question remains of historical interest and relevant to one's personal philosophy of life. But it is not the question before us, or that posed by nonviolent action. This is a question of the political potentialities of a technique of action which has in certain situations demonstrated its relevance and effectiveness.

No matter from what philosophical or ideological position one starts, there is no cut and dried answer concerning how this technique might be applied in a multitude of situations in which there is now widespread ultimate reliance on violence. There are no carefully worked out plans.

There is great need for research and analysis on this technique, and its possible relevance to the types of situations we have suggested. There is need for widespread study of the existing knowledge in the field, and for a public educational program (through the schools, political parties, religious bodies, peace groups, trade unions, etc.) on this possible response to the modern problem of political conflict.

Careful training is needed for those desiring to practice the technique in particular situations, and further experimental application of it will increase our knowledge of its nature and possibilities. Problems concerning its application, limitations and potentialities are inevitable. There is no blueprint. Success cannot be guaranteed, any more than it can by the use of other techniques.

Existing knowledge and experience, however, indicate that this is a direction which merits full consideration. In light of the severity of the problem posed by contemporary forms of political violence, this is a possible alternative which we dare not ignore.

Notes

1. Major General Olaf Helset, "Idrettsfronten," in Sverre Steen (gen. ed.), *Norges Krig,* Oslo, Gyldendal Norsk Forlag, 1947-50, vol. III, pp. 8-9.
2. *Ibid,* p. 9
3. *Ibid,* p. 14-15.
4. *Ibid,* p. 25.
5. *Ibid,* p. 7-8.
6. Thomas C. Wyller, *Nyordning og Motstand: Organisasjones Politiske Rolle Under Okkupasjonen* (Oslo, Universitetsforlaget, 1958). p. 11.
7. Magne Skodvin, "Det Store Fremstot," in Steen (gen. ed.), *Norges Krig,* Vol. II, pp. 640-641.
8. See Sharp, *Gandhi Wields the Weapon of Moral Power* (Ahmedabad, Navajivan, 1960), pp. 37-226; S. Gopal, *The Viceroyality of Lord Irwin, 1926-1931* (London,

Oxford University Press, 1957); pp. 54-122; and Simone Panter-Brick, *Gandhi Against Machiavellism* (Bombay, London, New York, *et al,* Asia Publishing House, 1966), pp. 135-154.

9. See Joan V. Bondurant, *Conquest of Violence: The Gandhian Philosophy of Conflict* (Berkely, University of California Press, 1965), pp. 46-52; M. K. Gandhi, *Non-violent Resistance* (New York, Schoken, 1967), pp. 46-52; and Mahadev Desai, *The Epic of Travancore* (Ahmedabad, Navajivan, 1937).

10. *The Inter-American,* Vol. III, No. 6 (June, 1944), p. 8.

11. *Newsweek,* issue of 22 May, 1944.

12. See also the account in Sharp, *The Politics of Nonviolent Action* (Philadelphia, Pilgrim Press, 1971) and listings in Bibliography.

13. For sources on this case, see items listed under Soviet prison camp strikes in the Bibliography.

14. See Martin Luther King, Jr., *Stride Toward Freedom* (New York, Harper & Row, 1958).

15. This account is based on a draft by Ronald McCarthy. See also Fulgencio Batista, *Cuba Betrayed* (New York, Vantage Press, 1962); Theodore Draper, *Castro's Revolution, Myths and Realities* (New York, Praeger, 1962); Ernesto Guevara, *Reminiscences of the Cuban Revolutionary War* (New York, Monthly Review Press, 1968); Earl E. T. Smith, *The Fourth Floor: An Account of the Castro Communist Revolution* (New York, Random House, 1962); and Robert Taber, *M-26: Biography of a Revolution* (New York, Lyle Stuart, 1961).

16. Ernesto Guevara, *Reminiscences of the Cuban Revolutionary War* (New York, Monthly Review Press, 1968), p. 242.

17. *Ibid,* p. 242 and Robert Taber, *op. cit,* p. 239.

18. Earl E. T. Smith, *op. cit.,* p. 189.

2

The Technique of Nonviolent Action

It is widely believed that military combat is the only effective means of struggle in a wide variety of situations of acute conflict. However, there is another whole approach to the waging of social and political conflict. Any proposed substitute for war in the defense of freedom must involve wielding power, confronting and engaging an invader's military might, and waging effective combat. The technique of nonviolent action, although relatively ignored and undeveloped, may be able to meet these requirements, and provide the basis for a defense policy.

Alternative Approach to the Control of Political Power
Military action is based largely on the idea that the most effective way of defeating an enemy is by inflicting heavy destruction on his armies, military equipment, transport system, factories and cities. Weapons are designed to kill or destroy with maximum efficiency. Nonviolent action is based on a different approach: to deny the enemy the human assistance and cooperation which are necessary if he is to exercise control over the population. It is thus based *29*

on a more fundamental and sophisticated view of political power.

A ruler's power is ultimately dependent on support from the people he would rule. His moral authority, economic resources, transport system, government bureaucracy, army and police – to name but a few immediate sources of his power – rest finally upon the cooperation and assistance of other people. If there is general conformity, the ruler is powerful.

But people do not always do what their rulers would like them to do. The factory manager recognizes this when he finds his workers leaving their jobs and machines, so that the production line ceases operation; or when he finds the workers persisting in doing something on the job which he has forbidden them to do. In many areas of social and political life comparable situations are commonplace. A man who has been a ruler and thought his power secure may discover that his subjects no longer believe he has any moral right to give them orders, that his laws are disobeyed, that the country's economy is paralyzed, that his soldiers and police are lax in carrying out repression or openly mutiny, and even that his bureaucracy no longer takes orders. When this happens, the man who has been ruler becomes simply another man, and his political power dissolves, just as the factory manager's power does when the workers no longer cooperate and obey. The equipment of his army may remain intact, his soldiers uninjured and very much alive, his cities unscathed, the factories and transport systems in full operational capacity, and the government buildings and offices unchanged. Yet because the human assistance which had created and supported his political power has been withdrawn, the former ruler finds that his political power has disintegrated.[1]

Nonviolent Action

The technique of nonviolent action, which is based on this approach to the control of political power and the waging of political struggles, has been the subject of many misconceptions: for the sake of clarity the two terms are defined in this section.

The term *technique* is used here to describe the over-all means of conducting an action or struggle. One can therefore speak of the technique of guerrilla warfare, of conventional warfare, and of parliamentary democracy.

The term *nonviolent action* refers to those methods of protest, noncooperation and intervention in which the actionists, without employing physical violence, refuse to do certain things which they are expected, or required, to do; or do certain things which they are not expected, or are forbidden, to do. In a particular case there can of course be a combination of acts of omission and acts of commission.

Nonviolent action is a generic term: it includes the large class of phenomena variously called nonviolent resisttance, satyagraha, passive resistance, positive action, and nonviolent direct action. While it is not violent, it *is* action, and not inaction; passivity, submission and cowardice must be surmounted if it is to be used. It is a means of conducting conflicts and waging struggles, and is not to be equated with (though it may be accompanied by) purely verbal dissent or solely psychological influence. It is not pacifism,[2] and in fact has in the vast majority of cases been applied by nonpacifists.[3] The motives for the adoption of nonviolent action may be religious or ethical, or they may be based on considerations of expediency. Nonviolent action is not an escapist approach to the problem of violence, for it can be applied in struggles against opponents relying on violent sanctions. The fact that in a conflict one side is nonviolent does not imply that the other side will also refrain from violence. Certain forms of nonviolent action may be regarded as efforts to persuade by action, while others are more coercive.

Methods of Nonviolent Action

There is a very wide range of methods, or forms, of nonviolent action, and at least 197 have been identified.[4] They fall into three classes — nonviolent protest and persuasion, noncooperation, and nonviolent intervention.

Generally speaking, the methods of *nonviolent protest* are symbolic in their effect and produce an awareness of the existence of dissent. Under tyrannical regimes, however, where opposition is stifled, their impact can in some circumstances be very great. Methods of nonviolent protest include marches, pilgrimages, picketing, vigils, "haunting" officials, public meetings, issuing and distributing protest literature, renouncing honors, protest emigration, and humorous pranks.

The methods of *nonviolent noncooperation,* if sufficient numbers take part, are likely to present the opponent with difficulties in maintaining the normal efficiency and operation of the system; and in extreme cases the system itself may be threatened. Methods of nonviolent noncooperation include various types of social noncooperation (such as social boycotts), economic boycotts (such as consumers' boycott, traders' boycott, rent refusal, and international trade embargo), strikes (such as the general strike, strike by resignation, industry strike, go-slow, and economic shutdown), and political noncooperation (such as boycott of government employment, boycott of elections, administrative noncooperation, civil disobedience, and mutiny).

The methods of *nonviolent intervention* have some features in common with the first two classes, but also challenge the opponent more directly; and, assuming that fearlessness and discipline are maintained, relatively small numbers may have a disproportionately large impact. Methods of nonviolent intervention include sit-ins, fasts, reverse strikes, nonviolent obstructions, nonviolent invasion, and parallel government.

The exact way in which methods from each of the three classes are combined varies considerably from one situa-

32

tion to another. Generally speaking, the risks to the actionists on the one hand, and to the system against which they take action on the other, are least in the case of nonviolent protest, and greatest in the case of nonviolent intervention. The methods of noncooperation tend to require the largest numbers, but not to demand a large degree of special training from all participants. The methods of nonviolent intervention are generally effective if the participants possess a high degree of internal discipline and are willing to accept severe repression; the tactics must also be selected and carried out with particular care and intelligence.

Several important factors need to be considered in the selection of the methods to be used in a given situation. These factors include the type of issue involved, the nature of the opponent, his aims and strength, the type of counter-action he is likely to use, the depth of feeling both among the general population and among the likely actionists, the degree of repression the actionists are likely to be able to take, the general strategy of the over-all campaign, and the amount of past experience and specific training the population and the actionists have had. Just as in military battle weapons are carefully selected, taking into account such factors as their range and effect, so also in nonviolent struggle the choice of specific methods is very important.

choice of tactics

Mechanisms of Change

In nonviolent struggles there are, broadly speaking, three mechanisms by which change is brought about. Usually there is a combination of the three. They are conversion, accommodation, and nonviolent coercion.

George Lakey has described the *conversion* mechanism thus: "By conversion we mean that the opponent, as the result of the actions of the nonviolent person or group, comes around to a new point of view which embraces the ends of the nonviolent actor."[5] This conversion can be influenced by reason or argument, but in nonviolent action it is also likely to be influenced by emotional and moral factors, which can in turn be stimulated by the suffering of the nonviolent actionists, who seek to achieve their goals without inflicting injury on other people.

Attempts at conversion, however, are not always successful, and may not even be made. *Accommodation* as a mechanism of nonviolent action falls in an intermediary position between conversion and nonviolent coercion, and elements of both of the other mechanisms are generally involved. In accommodation, the opponent, although not converted, decides to grant the demands of the nonviolent actionists in a situation where he still has a choice of action. The social situation within which he must operate has been altered enough by nonviolent action to compel a change in his own response to the conflict; perhaps because he has begun to doubt the rightness of his position, perhaps because he does not think the matter worth the trouble caused by the struggle, and perhaps because he anticipates coerced defeat and wishes to accede gracefully or with a minimum of losses.

Nonviolent coercion may take place in any of three circumstances. Defiance may become too widespread and massive for the ruler to be able to control it by repression; the social and political system may become paralyzed; or the extent of defiance or disobedience among the ruler's own soldiers and other agents may undermine his capacity to apply repression. Nonviolent coercion becomes possible when those applying nonviolent action succeed in withholding, directly or indirectly, the necessary sources of the ruler's political power. His power then disintegrates, and he is no longer able to control the situation, even though he still wishes to do so.

Nonviolent Action versus Violence

There can be no presumption that an opponent, faced
with an opposition relying solely on nonviolent methods,

will suddenly renounce his capacity for violence. Instead, nonviolent action can operate against opponents able and willing to use violent sanctions, and can counter their violence in such a way that they are thrown politically off balance in a kind of political *jiu-jitsu.*

Instead of confronting the opponent's police and troops with the same type of forces, nonviolent actionists counter these agents of the opponent's power indirectly. Their aim is to demonstrate that repression is incapable of cowing the populace, and to deprive the opponent of his existing support, thereby undermining his ability or will to continue with the repression. Far from indicating the failure of nonviolent action, repression often helps to make clear the cruelty of the political system being opposed, and so to alienate support from it. Repression is often a kind of recognition from the opponent that the nonviolent action constitutes a serious threat to his policy or regime, one which he finds it necessary to combat.

Just as in war danger from enemy fire does not always force front line soldiers to panic and flee, so in nonviolent action repression does not necessarily produce submission. True, repression *may* be effective, but it may fail to halt defiance, and in this case the opponent will be in difficulties. Repression against a nonviolent group which persists in face of it and maintains nonviolent discipline may have the following effects: it may alienate the general population from the opponent's regime, making them more likely to join the resistance; it may alienate the opponent's usual supporters and agents, and their initial uneasiness may grow into internal opposition and at times into noncooperation and disobedience; and it may rally general public opinion (domestic or international) to the support of the nonviolent actionists; though the effectiveness of this last factor varies greatly from one situation to another, it may produce various types of supporting actions. If repression thus produces larger numbers of nonviolent actionists, thereby increasing the defiance, and if it leads to internal dissent among the opponent's supporters, thereby reducing his capacity to deal with the defiance, it will clearly have rebounded against the opponent.

Naturally, with so many variables (including the nature of the contending groups, the issues involved, the context of the struggle, the means of repression, and the methods of nonviolent action used), in no two instances will nonviolent action "work" in exactly the same way. However, it is possible to indicate in very general terms the ways in which it does achieve results, It is, of course, sometimes defeated: no technique of action can guarantee its user short-term victory in every instance of its use. It is important to recognize, however, that failure in non-violent action may be caused, not by an inherent weakness of the technique, but by weakness in the movement employing it, or in the strategy and tactics used.

Strategy is just as important in nonviolent action as it is in military action. While military strategic concepts and principles cannot be automatically carried over into the field of nonviolent struggle, since the dynamics and mechanisms of military and nonviolent action differ greatly, the basic importance of strategy and tactics is in no way diminished. The attempt to cope with strategic and tactical problems associated with civilian defense (national defense by prepared nonviolent resistance) therefore needs to be based on thorough consideration of the dynamics and mechanisms of nonviolent struggle; and on consideration of the general principles of strategy and tactics appropriate to the technique – both those peculiar to it and those which may be carried over from the strategy of military and other types of conflict.

The Indirect Approach to the Opponent's Power

The technique of nonviolent action, and the policy of civilian defense relying upon it, can be regarded as extreme forms of the "strategy of indirect approach" which Liddell

Hart has propounded in the sphere of military strategy. He has argued that a direct strategy — confronting the opponent head-on — consolidates the opponent's strength. "To move along the line of natural expectation consolidates the opponent's balance and thus increases his resisting power." An indirect approach, he argues, is militarily more sound, and generally effective results have followed when the plan of action has had "such indirectness as to ensure the opponent's unreadiness to meet it." "Dislocation" of the enemy is crucial, he insists, to achieve the conditions for victory, and the dislocation must be followed by "exploitation" of the opportunity created by the position of insecurity. It thus becomes important "to nullify opposition by paralyzing the power to oppose," and to make "the enemy do something wrong."[6]

These general, and at first glance abstract, principles of strategy can take a concrete form not only in certain types of military action, but also in nonviolent action, and therefore in civilian defense. An invader, or other usurper, is likely to be best equipped to apply, and to combat, military and other violent means of combat and repression. Instead of meeting him directly on that level, nonviolent actionists and civilian defenders rely on a totally different technique of struggle, or "weapons system." The whole conflict takes on a very special character: the combatants fight, but with different weapons. Given an extensive, determined and skilful application of nonviolent action, the opponent is likely to find that the nonviolent actionists' insistence on fighting with their chosen "weapons system" will cause him very special problems which frustrate the effective utilization of his own forces. As indicated above, the opponent's unilateral use of violent repression may only increase the resistance and win new support for the resisters; and even the opponent's supporters, agents and soldiers may first begin to doubt the rightness of his policies, and finally undertake internal opposition.

The use of nonviolent action may thus reduce or remove the very sources of the opponent's power without ever directly confronting him with the same violent means of action on which he had relied. The course of the struggle may be viewed as an attempt by the nonviolent actionists to increase their various types of strength, not only among their usual supporters but also among third parties and in the opponent's camp, and to reduce by various processes the strength of the opponent. This type of change in the relative power positions will finally determine the outcome of the struggle.

Success in nonviolent struggle depends to a very high degree on the persistence of the nonviolent actionists in fighting with *their own* methods, and opposing all pressures — whether caused by emotional hostility to the opponent's brutalities, temptations of temporary gains, or *agents provocateurs* employed by the opponent (of which there have been examples) — to fight with the opponent's own, violent, methods. Violence by, or in support of, their side will sharply counter the operation of the very special mechanisms of change in nonviolent action — even when the violence is on a relatively small scale, such as rioting, injury, violent sabotage involving loss of life, or individual assassinations. The least amount of violence will, in the eyes of many, justify severe repression, and it will sharply reduce the tendency for such repression to bring sympathy and support for the nonviolent actionists; and it may well, for several reasons, reduce the number of resisters. Violence will also sharply reduce sympathy and support in the opponent's own camp.

The use of violence by, or in support of, the resisters, has many effects. Its dangers are indicated by, among other things, an examination of the likely effect on the opponent's soldiers and police, who may have become sympathetic to the resisters and reluctant to continue as opposition agents. It is well known that ordinary soldiers will fight more persistently and effectively if it is a matter of survival, and if they and their comrades are being shot, bombed, wounded, or killed. Soldiers and police acting against a nonviolent opposition and not facing such dangers may at times be inefficient in carrying out repression — for example by slackness in searches for "wanted" resisters, firing over the heads of demonstrators, or not shooting at all. In extreme cases they may openly mutiny. When such inefficiency or mutiny occurs, the opponent's power is severely threatened; this will often be an objective of nonviolent actionists or civilian defenders.

The introduction of violence by their side, however, will sharply reduce their chances of undermining opposition loyalty, as the influences producing sympathy are removed and their opponents' lives become threatened. This is simply an illustration of the point that it is very dangerous to believe that one can increase one's total combat strength by combining violent sabotage, assassinations, or types of guerrilla or conventional warfare, with civilian defense, which relies on the very different technique of nonviolent action.

Development of the Technique

Nonviolent action has a long history, but because historians have often been more concerned with other matters much information has undoubtedly been lost. Even today, this field is largely ignored, and there is no good history of the practice and development of the technique. But it clearly began early. For example, in 494 BC the plebeians of Rome, rather than murder the Consuls, withdrew from the city to the Sacred Mount where they remained for some days, thereby refusing to make their usual contribution to the life of the city, until an agreement was reached pledging significant improvements in their life and status.[7]

A very significant pre-Gandhian expansion of the technique took place in the nineteenth and early twentieth centuries. The technique received impetus from three groups during this period: first from trade unionists and other social radicals who sought a means of struggle — largely strikes, general strikes and boycotts — against what they regarded as an unjust social system, and for an improvement in the condition of working men; second, from nationalists who found the technique useful in resisting a foreign enemy — such as the Hungarian resistance against Austria between 1850 and 1867, and the Chinese boycotts of Japanese goods in the early twentieth century; and third, on the level of ideas and personal example, from individuals, such as Leo Tolstoi in Russia and Henry David Thoreau in the USA, who wanted to show how a better society might be created.[8]

While the use of nonviolent action by trade unionists and nationalists contributed significantly to its development, little attention was given to the refinement and improvement of the technique. Practical nonviolent struggle sometimes took passive forms and, on occasion, very militant, even interventionist forms. Religious groups like the early Quakers had practiced nonviolent action as a corporate as well as an individual reaction to persecution; but the corporate practice of this technique by nonreligious groups was almost unrelated to the idea that nonviolent behavior was morally preferable to violent behavior.

With Gandhi's experiments in the use of nonviolent action to control rulers, alter policies, and undermine political systems, the character of the technique was broadened and refinements were made in its practice. Many modifications were introduced: greater attention was given to strategy and tactics; the armory of methods was expanded; and a link was consciously forged between mass political action and the ethical principle of nonviolence. Gandhi, with his political colleagues and fellow Indians, demonstrated in a variety of conflicts in South Africa and India that nonviolent struggle could be
politically effective on a large scale. He termed his

refinement of the technique "satyagraha," meaning roughly insistence and reliance upon the power of truth. "In politics, its use is based upon the immutable maxim, that government of the people is possible only so long as they consent either consciously or unconsciously to be governed."[9] While he sought to convert the British, he did not imagine that there could be an easy solution which would not necessitate struggle and the exercise of power. Just before the beginning of the 1930-31 civil disobedience campaign he wrote to the Viceroy:

> It is not a matter of carrying conviction by argument. The matter resolves itself into one of matching forces. Conviction or no conviction, Great Britain would defend her Indian commerce and interests by all the forces at her command. India must consequently evolve force enough to free herself from that embrace of death.[10]

Since Gandhi's time, the use of nonviolent action has spread throughout the world at an unprecedented rate. In some cases it was stimulated by Gandhi's thought and practice, but where this was so the technique was often modified in new cultural and political settings; in these cases it has already moved beyond Gandhi.

Quite independently of the campaigns led by Gandhi, important nonviolent struggles emerged under exceedingly difficult circumstances in Nazi-occupied and Communist countries: nonviolent action was used to a significant extent in the Norwegian and Danish resistance in the Second World War, in the East German uprising in 1953, in the Hungarian revolution in 1956, and in the strikes in the Soviet political prisoner camps, especially in 1953. There have been other important developments in Africa, Japan, and elsewhere. There have, of course, been setbacks, and the limited and sporadic use of nonviolent action in South Africa, for example, has been followed by advocacy of *41* violence.[11] However, when seen in historical perspective, there is no doubt that the technique of nonviolent action has developed very rapidly in the twentieth century.

In this same perspective, it is only recently that nonviolent resistance has been seen as a possible substitute for war in deterring or defeating invasion and other threats. It is even more recently that any attempt has been made to work out this policy — now called 'civilian defense' — in any detail, and that an examination of its merits and problems has been proposed.

It is inconceivable that any country will in the foreseeable future permanently abandon its defensive capacity. Threats — some genuine, some exaggerated — are too real to people; there has been too much aggression and seizure of power by dictators to be forgotten. But while defense and deterrence inevitably rely on sanctions and means of struggle, there is much reason for dissatisfaction with the usual military means. The question therefore arises whether there exists an alternative means of struggle which could be the basis of a new defense policy. Nonviolent action is an alternative means of struggle: in this, it has more in common with military struggle than with conciliation and arbitration. Could there then be a policy of civilian defense which relies on this nonviolent technique? The question must be answered, not in terms of philosophy and dogma, but in the practical examination of concrete strategies through which it might operate, the problems which might be faced, and alternative ways in which these might possibly be solved. All this will depend to a large degree on an understanding of the technique of nonviolent action, its methods, dynamics, mechanisms, and requirements.

Learning From the Past

Generally speaking, very little effort has been made to learn from past cases of nonviolent action with a view to increasing our understanding of the nature of the technique, and gaining knowledge which might be useful in future struggles, or which might contribute to an expansion of the use of nonviolent action instead of violence. Study of past cases could provide the basis for a more informed assessment of the future political potentialities of the technique.

There are far too few detailed documentary accounts of past uses of nonviolent action; such accounts can provide raw material for analyses of particular facets of the technique and help in the formulation of hypotheses which might be tested in other situations. An important step, therefore, in the development of research in this field is the preparation of purely factual accounts of a large number of specific cases of nonviolent action, accompanied if possible with collections of existing interpretations and explanations of the events.

A compilation of as many instances of socially or politically significant nonviolent action as can be discovered is also needed, and should preferably include a few standard major facts about the cases, and bibliographic clues. Such a survey could help in the selection of the cases meriting more detailed investigation; and it would make possible more authoritative comparisons of the cases with particular factors in mind, such as the geographical, historical, and cultural distribution of the cases, the types of issues involved, and the types of opponents against whom nonviolent struggles have been waged.

Another subject which deserves careful study is the meaning of, and conditions for, success in nonviolent action. The varying meanings of the terms "success" and "defeat" need to be distinguished, and consideration given to concrete achievements in particular struggles. The matter is much more complex than may at first appear. For example, failure within a short period of time to get an invader to withdraw fully from an occupied country may nevertheless be accompanied by the frustration of several of the invader's objectives, the maintenance of a considerable degree of autonomy within the "conquered" country, and the furtherance of a variety of changes in the invader's own regime and homeland; these changes may themselves later lead either to the desired full withdrawal, or to further relaxation of occupation rule. When various types of "success" and "defeat" have been distinguished, it would be desirable to have a study of the conditions under which they have occurred in the past and seem possible in the future. These conditions would include factors in the social and political situation, the nature of the issues in the conflict, the type of opponent and his repression, the type of group using nonviolent action, the type of nonviolent action used (taking into account quality, extent, strategy, tactics, methods, persistence in face of repression, etc.), and lastly the possible role and influence of "third parties."

The question of the viability and political practicality of the technique of nonviolent action is one which can be investigated by research and analysis, and it is possible that the efficiency and political potentialities of this technique can be increased by deliberate efforts. The question of violent or nonviolent means in politics and defense, if tackled in this manner, is removed from the sphere of "belief" or "nonbelief" and opened up for investigation and research.

NOTES

1. For a fuller discussion of this approach to political power, see Sharp, *The Politics of Nonviolent Action,* Chapter 1 (Philadelphia, Pilgrim Press, 1971).
2. For a definition of "pacifism," see Sharp, *An Abecedary of Nonviolent Action and Civilian Defense* (Cambridge, Mass., Schenkman, 1970).
3. See the discussion of "85 cases of Nonviolent Action" in this book.
4. See Sharp, *The Politics of Nonviolent Action.*
5. George Lakey, "The Sociological Mechanisms of Nonviolent Action," *Peace Research Reviews,* Oakville, Ontario, Canadian Peace Research Institute Vol. II, No. 6 (Dec., 1968).
6. B. H. Liddel Hart, *Strategy: The Indirect Approach* (London, Faber and Faber, 1954), pp. 25, 349, 359, and 350. (Also published under the title *Strategy,* by New York, Praeger, 1954.)
7. See F. R. Cowell, *The Revolutions of Ancient Rome* (London, Thames and Hudson, 1962, and New York, Praeger, 1963, pp. 42-43). Cowell's account is based on Livy.
8. See Leo Tolstoi, *The Kingdom of God Is Within You* (New York, Thomas Y. Crowell, 1899, and London, William Heineman, 1894); and Henry David Thoreau, *On the Duty of Civil Disobedience* (1849), introduction by Gene Sharp (London, Peace News Pamphlet, 1963).
9. M. K. Gandhi, *Indian Opinion* (Golden Number, 1914). Quoted in Gandhi, *Satyagraha* (Ahmedabad, Navajivan, 1951), p. 35. (Also published under the title *Non-violent Resistance* (New York, Schocken Books, 1961.)
10. All-India Congress Committee, *Congress Bulletin* (March 7, 1930, No. 5). Quoted in Sharp, *Gandhi*

Wields the Weapon of Moral Power (Navajivan, Ahmedabad, 1960), p. 64. For a brief discussion of some popular misconceptions about Gandhi and his activities, see Sharp, "Gandhi's Political Significance Today," in G. Ramachandran and T. K. Mahadevan (eds.), *Gandhi: His Relevance for Our Times* (Bharatiya Vidya Bhavan, Bombay, 1964), pp. 44-66.

11. For a discussion of the strategic problems of resistance in South Africa and the potentialities of nonviolent action there, see Sharp, "Can Nonviolence Work in South Africa?", "Problems of Violent and Nonviolent Struggle," "Strategic Problems of the South African Resistance," and "How Do You Get Rid of Oppression?" in *Peace News* (London, June 21, June 28, July 5, and October 25, 1963).

3

National Defense Without Armaments

Now, more than ever, we need to question some of our basic assumptions about defense, security and peace, and to examine possible new policies that might help achieve those goals. The dangers and limitations of modern military means — conventional, nuclear, and chemical-bacteriological — are too obvious to need repetition. What has not been clear is what alternative we have. This chapter is focused on one alternative system of defense, which is most commonly called civilian defense.

The often-posed choice between the acceptance of tyranny and the waging of war has been aggravated by developments in weapons technology, communications, and transportation. The technological changes in methods of war have brought about the concentration of large-scale military power in the hands of a few countries which possess scientific know-how, a technological and industrial base, and vast resources. In particular, the supremacy of the United States and the Soviet Union in capability for large-scale conventional and nuclear warfare cannot yet be seriously challenged.

In consequence, most countries have found that their capacity for self-defense has been drastically reduced or destroyed altogether. This is true even for highly industrialized Western European countries, and the matter is more extreme for less developed countries.

At the same time, local conflicts have gained worldwide significance and led to direct involvement in one form or another by the super powers. This gravitation of deterrence and defense tasks to the most powerful and most technologically developed countries has had a variety of undesirable results for the other countries.

For example, alliance with a super power is no sure guarantee of national security. The ultimate defense decision lies in foreign hands, and despite treaties a small power may be left helpless when the chips are down, as the fate of Czechoslovakia in 1939 illustrated. In 1968, Czechoslovakia was attacked by its own allies!

Likewise, military help from a super power can be highly dangerous for the people being "defended." Witness Vietnam. And what would happen to West Berlin, or even West Germany, in case of powerful American military help to throw back a Russian invasion?

Dependence on stronger powers for defense may have other disadvantages. For example, do not the very people who want American military support frequently resent being dependent on it? Does not dependence on others for defense sometimes lead to reduced willingness to contribute to one's own defense? Does not such dependence often lead to an unwise stifling of one's own political judgment and autonomy in both domestic and foreign policies?

This shift of responsibility for the security of many nations to the super powers has more than doubled the latter's defense tasks. Military commitments of the U.S. extend far beyond its own defense. Dozens of countries around the world depend on American support and pledges for their security. A similar situation exists on a smaller scale for the Soviet Union. Someday China may have a comparable status.

These foreign commitments (assuming good motives behind them) are for the United States an extraordinarily difficult and often thankless task. Even from a military perspective, there are severe problems involved in carrying out this world role.

The political problems are also severe. It is hard, for example, to pose as a defender of freedom when that role seems to require alliances with reactionary dictatorships. Great sacrifices intended to help people avoid dictatorial rule are sometimes seen as unwanted efforts of Uncle Sam to be the world's policeman. Or, less flatteringly, as ruthless attempts to impose a new imperialism.

The Need for Self-defense

It is hardly necessary to mention that the local involvement of a super power carries with it the additional danger of escalation into a larger international war. All this is to say nothing of the drain of resources on the United States, the killing of American soldiers, the effects of such violence abroad on the society at home, or the distraction from other important domestic and international tasks.

This could all be changed if countries fearing military aggression or the imposition by violence of minority dictatorships had the capacity to defend themselves – in other words, if countries throughout the world were able, primarily by their own efforts, to defeat domestic or foreign-aided dictatorial groups of *any* political stripe, and also were able to deter and defeat international aggression against themselves.

The world security situation would then be very different, and would not "require" global American military involvement. There would then be neither the need nor the excuse for worldwide military commitments of the United States or any other country. The super powers could instead concentrate on their own defenses and devote their technical and financial superiority to constructive humanitarian ends.

But is this possible? How can the capacity for self-defense be restored, if it has been destroyed by the very nature of modern military technology? We need to ask: Can there be a new concept of defense which is *not* dependent on military technology, but which could nevertheless be effective against real dangers? That could only happen if defense could be provided *without* military means — an idea inconceivable to most people.

Defense has almost always meant military defense. I will argue that this need no longer be true. The main question is: How can there be a nonmilitary defense?

We must start with basics. We have usually assumed that defense capacity and military power are identical, and that military occupation means political control. But these assumptions are not valid:

1. Military power today often exists without real capacity to *defend* in struggle the people and society relying upon it. Often it only threatens mutual annihilation. More importantly — and this is the main argument of this article — defense capacity can today be provided without military means.

2. Military occupation does *not* necessarily give the invader political control of the country, and the occupation can be destroyed *without* military resistance.

Direct Defense by Civilians

Since military technology in most cases has abolished the possibility of effective geographical defense, we are thrown back to the people for the defense of their freedoms and society. This approach is called *civilian defense* (not to be confused with civil defense).

Civilian defense aims to defeat military aggression by using resistance by the civilian population as a whole to make it impossible for the enemy to establish and maintain political control over the country. This is a direct defense of the society by the citizens. The priorities of action are crucial. The maintenance of a free press, for example, or keeping the invader's propaganda out of the schools is each of more direct importance to democracy than, say, possession of a given mountain or the killing of young conscripts in the invader's army. Large-scale preparations and training would be necessary to maximize the effectiveness of social, economic and political power against an invader or an internal take-over.

The citizens would prevent enemy control of the country by massive and selective refusal to cooperate and to obey, supporting instead the legal government and its call to resist. For example, police would refuse to locate and arrest patriotic opponents of the invader. Teachers would refuse to introduce his propaganda into the schools — as happened in Norway under the Nazis. Workers and managers would use strikes, delays and obstructionism to impede exploitation of the country — as happened in the Ruhr in 1923. Clergymen would preach about the duty to refuse to help the invader — as happened in the Netherlands under the Nazis.

Politicians, civil servants and judges, by ignoring or defying the enemy's illegal orders, would keep the normal machinery of government and the courts out of his control — as happened in the German resistance to the Kapp *Putsch* in 1920. Newspapers refusing to submit to censorship would be published illegally in large editions or many small editions — as happened in the Russian 1905 Revolution and in several Nazi-occupied countries. Free radio programs would continue from hidden transmitters — as happened in Czechoslovakia in August, 1968.

In civilian defense struggles, the general citizenry and the society's institutions are themselves combatants. When successful, civilian defense of the society would lead to the collapse or withdrawal of the invader or internal usurper. But the victory would follow from the successful direct defense of the society, not from battles over the control of geography.

In addition, in case of invasion, civilian defense would set in motion restraining influences both in the invader's own country (stimulating dissension at home, splits in the regime, and, in extremes, even resistance) and in the international community (creating diplomatic pressures, political losses, and sometimes economic sanctions) that would be inimical to the invader's interests and to his attempts at consolidating an occupation.

This may sound unlikely. But there is more evidence that civilian defense can work than there was 30 years ago for the practicability of nuclear weapons, intercontinental rockets and trips to the moon.

Nevertheless, the idea that national defense may be exercised more effectively by the vigilance and trained nonviolent resistance of citizens than by military means seems startling to some and ridiculous to others. There is no denying that there would be risks and dangers involved in such a policy. But these need to be measured against the risks and dangers of the military deterrence policies currently in operation.

The Need for Critical Examination

Contrary to present assumptions, there is a long history of nonviolent political struggle. Despite lack of knowledge of its requirements, and in the absence of training and preparations, this technique has produced some impressive results, even against high odds.

There are as yet no cases in which prepared civilian defense has caused an invader to withdraw — because there has never yet been a case of prepared civilian defense being used as a country's official defense policy. (There are, of course, cases of effective unprepared resistance in occupied countries, such as colonial India and World War II Norway.) The formulation of a civilian defense policy is a deliberate attempt to advance beyond where we are now, an attempt based upon a serious calculation of political realities and possibilities.

Given the resources and the commitment, there is reason to believe progress can be made in devising political strategies of nonviolent action calculated to control tyrants and preserve political freedom. With political research and analysis, it seems to me that we could locate and come to understand the weaknesses of occupation regimes and of totalitarian systems. Then we could concentrate resistance against them on their weak points, using what might be called a form of "political *karate*."

Even *without* advance preparations, the people of Czechoslovakia provided an experiment in the use of nonviolent struggle in their response to the Russian invasion and occupation. Given the options open to them, their successes, while moderate, were temporarily impressive. The Russians have not yet withdrawn; they have won for the moment, although at greater cost than expected. The Dubcek regime held out from August until April, while the Russians expected to be able to overcome possible Czech military resistance within days. We need to learn from the strengths and weaknesses of this case.

Civilian defense ought to be subjected to an examination and consideration at least as rigorous as that devoted to any proposal for a major change in defense policy. Concrete examination has to be given to the many practical problems involved in waging civilian defense, to possible strategies, to types of repression that would need to be anticipated, and to the question of the casualties. My plea, therefore, is not for the adoption of civilian defense now, but for research, investigation and official consideration. My intent is not to win converts, but to provoke thought.

Begin With the Known
As a first step, civilian defense must draw upon the known experience of nonviolent struggle, without being limited by it, in order to develop viable strategies to deter and defeat attacks on a country.   *53*

The study of cases of nonviolent action has been largely neglected by strategists, historians and social scientists. Serious research to correct this neglect has only begun. Moreover, the situation has been aggravated by a series of misunderstandings about the nature of nonviolent action which need to be corrected.

Nonviolent action, the major instrument of a civilian defense policy, is the opposite of passivity and cowardice. It is not simply persuasion, but the wielding of power. It does not assume that man is inherently "good." It has been mostly used by "ordinary" people. It does not absolutely require shared principles or a high degree of common interest between the contending groups. It may work by "nonviolent coercion." *At least* as "Western" as it is "Eastern," the technique is designed for struggle against a repressive violent opponent. It may be used to defend as well as to change a government, and has been widely applied against foreign occupations and even against totalitarian systems.

There are many instances of effective nonviolent action, including: the early resistance by American colonists, 1763-1775; Hungarian passive resistance vs. Austrian rule, especially 1850-1867; Finland's disobedience and political noncooperation against Russia, 1898-1905; the Russian 1905 Revolution, and that of February, 1917 (before the October Bolshevik *coup*); the Korean nonviolent protest against Japanese rule, 1919-1922 (which failed); the Indian 1930-1931 independence campaign; German government-sponsored resistance to the Franco-Belgian occupation of the Ruhr in 1923.

Later examples include: resistance in several Nazi-occupied countries, especially Norway, the Netherlands and Denmark; governmental and popular measures to nullify anti-Jewish measures in several Nazi-allied and Nazi-occupied countries, such as Bulgaria, Italy, France and Denmark; the toppling by popular noncooperation *54* and defiance of the dictators of El Salvador and Guatemala in 1944; the 1963 and 1966 campaigns of the Buddhists against the Saigon regimes in South Vietnam.

Other recent cases involve resistance, uprisings and less dramatic pressures for liberalization in communist-ruled countries, including the 1953 East German uprising, strikes in the Soviet political prisoner camps in 1953, major aspects of the 1956 Hungarian revolution, Polish popular pressures for reforms, efforts for de-Stalinization in the Soviet Union, popular pressures for liberalization in Czechoslovakia early in 1968 and popular and governmental noncooperation following the Russian invasion in August.

Thus, it is evident that nonviolent resistance has occurred even against totalitarian systems, on an improvised basis and despite the absence of training, preparations and know-how. It should be noted that totalitarians like Hitler deliberately sought to promote the impression of their regime's omnipotence, both domestically and internationally, to discourage any potential opposition. Such systems contain critical weaknesses in the form of inefficiencies, internal conflicts and tendencies toward impermanence. It is precisely these features that offer themselves up for exploitation by civilian defense strategies. However, the basic reason why civilian defense can be effective against totalitarian systems is that even such extreme political systems cannot free themselves entirely from dependence on their subjects. As an articulated strategy, civilian defense is designed to deny totalitarian rulers the compliance, cooperation and submission they require.

About 197 specific methods of nonviolent action have been identified. These methods are classified under three broad categories: protest, noncooperation and intervention, as noted briefly in the preceding chapter.

The methods of nonviolent protest are largely symbolic demonstrations, including parades, marches and vigils (54 methods). Noncooperation is divided into three sub-   *55* categories: a) social noncooperation (15 methods), b) economic noncooperation, including boycotts (26 methods) and strikes (23 methods), and c) acts of political noncooperation (38 methods). "Nonviolent intervention," by psychological, physical, social, economic, or political means, includes 40 methods (such as the fast, nonviolent occupation, and parallel government).

The use of a considerable number of these methods — carefully chosen, on a large scale, persistently, with wise strategy and tactics, by trained civilians — is likely to cause any illegitimate regime severe problems.

Nonviolent action resembles military war more than it does negotiation; it is a technique of struggle. As such, nonviolent action involves the use of power, but in different ways than military violence. Instead of confronting the opponent's apparatus of violence with comparable forces, the nonviolent actionists counter with political weapons. The degree to which noncooperation will threaten the opponent's power position varies, but its potential is best illustrated in the disruptive effects of massive strikes and in mutinies of the opponent's troops.

The violent antagonist's repressive measures are hardly insignificant, but *in themselves* they are not decisive. In fact, the opponent's repression is evidence of the power of nonviolent action, and is no more reason for despair than if, in a regular war, the enemy shoots back.

If the civilian defenders maintain their discipline and persist despite repression, and if they involve significant sections of the populace in the struggle, the opponent's will can be retarded and finally blocked. If leaders are arrested, the movement may carry on without a recognizable leadership. The opponent may declare new acts illegal, only to find that he has opened up new opportunities for defiance.

There is a strong tendency for the opponent's violence and repression to react against his power position. This is called "political *jiu-jitsu*." Against disciplined and persistent nonviolent actionists, his violence can never really come to grips with the kind of power they wield. Under certain conditions repression may make more people join the resistance. The opponent's supporters may turn against him; uneasiness may lead to disobedience in his own camp. The numbers of resisters may become so large that control becomes impossible. His police may give up, his officials occasionally resign, and sometimes his troops may even mutiny. Massive nonviolent defiance by the population has by then made the enemy government powerless. This is the potential. But it will not be easy to achieve. Defeat of the nonviolent actionists is always possible, just as defeat occurs in traditional war. Victory with this technique will come only to those who have developed it into a refined and powerful political tool.

Transarmament

Thus, civilian defense depends primarily on a trained civilian population to defend the country's freedom and independence by social, psychological, economic and political means. The population could be prepared through regular democratic processes and government decisions. Long before the change-over from military defense to civilian defense – a process called *transarmament* – considerable research, investigation, and analysis would be needed. Highly important, too, would be widespread public study, thinking, discussion and debate on the nature, feasibility, merits, and problems of civilian defense and all of the forms its exercise might take.

After the decision to transarm, a Department of Civilian Defense might be set up to provide planning, analysis, coordination and some leadership. All this would probably be more complex than planning for military defense.

No country is going to abandon military defense without confidence in a substitute defense policy. Therefore, for a significant period, civilian defense preparations would be carried out alongside military measures, until the 57 latter could be phased out as no longer needed. Because of their different natures, however, the two policies would probably require separate institutional arrangements. During the transarmament period, personnel and money would be needed for both.

A major educational program for the whole country on the nature and purpose of civilian defense would be required. Federal, state and local governmental bodies, assisted by independent institutions such as schools, churches, trade unions, business groups, newspapers, television and the like could undertake this. People would be informed about the broad outlines of the new policy, the ways it would operate, and the results expected.

Certain occupational groups, including those wishing to participate in advanced aspects of the policy, would need specialized training. Such training would vary in its character and purpose, ranging from that required by local neighborhood defense workers to specialist education at civilian defense counterparts of West Point. This is not to say that there is no role for spontaneity within the scope of civilian defense, but that it is a limited role and even then needs to be self-disciplined and rooted in thorough understanding of the requirements of nonviolent action and the chosen civilian defense strategies.

In crises, specialists in civilian defense would play an important role in initiating resistance, especially at the beginning of an occupation or a *coup*. In various situations they could serve as special cadres for particularly dangerous tasks. Some specialists might be kept in reserve to guide the later stages of the resistance. However, they could not — and should not be expected to — carry out the resistance *for* the general population. Responsibility for the main thrust of civilian defense must be assumed by the citizenry. Since the leaders generally would be among the first imprisoned or otherwise incapacitated by the usurper, the population must be able to continue on its own

initiative.

Maximizing Impact

Preparations for civilian defense would not consist simply of instructions arrived at by a centralized leadership and carried out at the lower levels. An effective strategy would require an analysis of the potentialities of many factors — means of transportation, government departments, schools, and so forth — to identify the specific points at which noncooperation might have a maximum impact in preventing any illegal group from seizing control. Ordinary people in jobs at those places would often be the best sources of the intelligence information needed to make these decisions. To make accurate tactical judgments, however, one would need knowledge of the forms and strategies of nonviolent resistance, the enemy's weaknesses, the kinds of repression to expect, the crucial political issues on which to resist, and many practical questions of how to implement the resistance.

The setting up of an underground system of contacts would probably have to wait until a crisis, to make it harder for the opponent to know the exact personnel and structure of the resistance organization. However, "war games" and civilian defense maneuvers could offer the specialists a chance to examine the viability of alternative strategies and tactics for dealing with various types of threats. Training maneuvers in which imaginary occupations or takeovers would be met by civilian resistance could be acted out at levels ranging from local residential areas, offices or factories to cities, states and even the whole country.

Technical preparations would also be necessary for civilian defense. For example, provisions and equipment would be required for communication with the population after the enemy had occupied key centers and seized established newspapers, radio stations and other mass media. Equipment to publish underground newspapers and resistance leaflets and to make broadcasts could be hidden *59* beforehand. It might be possible to make advance arrangements for locating such broadcasting stations or printing plants in the territory of a friendly neighboring country as part of a civilian defense mutual aid agreement.

Since an enemy might seek to force the population into submission by starvation, and since certain resistance methods (e.g., a general strike) would disrupt distribution of food, emergency supplies of staples should be stored locally. Alternative means of providing fuel and water during emergencies could also be explored. For certain types of crises, plans might be considered for the dispersal of large groups of people from big cities to rural areas where the oppressor would find it more difficult to exercise control over them.

Because civilian defense requires the active support and participation of the populace (*not* necessarily unanimity, however), the citizens must have both the *will* and *ability* to defend their society in crises. For citizens to have the will to defend their democratic system does not imply that they believe the system is perfect. But it does mean that the system is preferable to any regime likely to be imposed by internal take-over or by foreign invaders, and that any necessary changes in the system should be made by democratic decision. For effective civilian defense, people have to *want* to resist threats to their freedom and independence. They must genuinely cherish the democratic qualities of their society.

Measures to increase the effectiveness of civilian defense (including the decentralization of control in order to make citizens more self-reliant in facing emergencies) are likely to contribute to the vitality of democratic society, and to increased participation in it. With civilian defense, therefore, there is no rivalry or contradiction between defense requirements and domestic needs; they are complementary. In the case of the U.S., this would be a considerable advance over present military policy, which has delivered us into exactly that contradiction.

Civilian defense is thus a democratic defense of democracy. Just as tyranny and war, in their cyclical appearances, may be mutually-reinforcing causes, so political freedom and peace may be intimately connected. A civilian defense policy may provide concrete means for producing a condition of life that allows for the interplay and perpetual renewal of the last two qualities in place of the first two.

Aggressor's Considerations

An aggressive regime deciding whether or not to invade another country will usually consider: 1) the expected ease or difficulty of the invasion and subsequent control of the country, and 2) the anticipated gains as compared to costs (human, economic, political, ideological, prestigial, military, and other). Except in the case of a nation acting on a huge gamble or pure irrationality, the likelihood of considerably greater losses than gains will probably deter the invader.

Invasion is not an objective in and of itself. It is a way to achieve a wider purpose, which almost always involves occupation of the invaded country. If, however, a successful invasion is followed by immense difficulties in occupying and controlling the country, its society and population, the invasion's "success" becomes for its perpetrators a dangerous mirage. Certainly the Russians invading Czechoslovakia encountered at the early stages great and unanticipated difficulites. Advance civilian defense preparations and training could have considerably increased these. Where preparations and training are thorough, a would-be invader might perceive that he will not be able to rule successfully the country that he might easily invade. Civilian defense has at that moment revealed itself as a powerful deterrent.

There are other contingencies a would-be aggressor would need to think through. A population's spirit and methods of resistance could well spread to other countries *61* and again be applied against his tyranny. In such a light, civilian defense has to be considered as a possible post-nuclear deterrent to conventional attack.

Could civilian defense deter a nuclear attack? It is sometimes argued that civilian defense is nonsense in the nuclear age, since it would provide no defense should nuclear bombs start falling. The question, however, is whether the conditions likely to be produced by trans-armament to civilian defense will encourage or discourage launching a nuclear attack on the country involved.

Deterrence and Defense

Who fears and expects a nuclear attack the most today, and who the least? It is precisely the nuclear powers who most fear nuclear attack, partly because each side is afraid of the other. Brazil, Mexico, Indonesia, Canada and Australia — all *without* nuclear weapons — fear and expect nuclear attack far less than the U.S. and U.S.S.R.

Fear of nuclear attack, then, or fear of military defeat in a major conventional war, may be a strong reason for launching a nuclear attack on the enemy. Civilian defense, which can only be used for *defensive* purposes, would remove that motive, and hence, if not cancel out the danger, at least greatly reduce it. It is certainly significant that several military men to whom this problem has been presented do not see much likelihood of a nuclear attack against a country employing only civilian defense as a deterrent.

No deterrent can ever be *guaranteed* to deter. And, of course, the failure of the nuclear deterrent could permanently end all talk of alternative deterrents as well as the talkers and nontalkers. But the failure of the civilian defense deterrent would still permit human life to continue and long range hope for a just solution to remain, while the struggle against tyranny would enter a new stage with a more direct confrontation of forces. When the deterrence capacity of civilian defense fails, a series of contingency plans to deal with the new situation comes into operation with the potential to win a real political and human victory.

Although resistance is never easy, it is less difficult to resist a tyrannical regime while it is seeking to establish itself than after it has succeeded. George Kennan points out that for a successful seizure of power by a totalitarian regime "a certain degree of mass bewilderment and passivity are required." Advance preparations and training for civilian defense are designed specifically to prevent that condition. The invader will encounter a population well prepared to fight for its freedom with methods which, precisely because they are nonviolent, will be especially insidious and dangerous to the occupation regime. And in the end, the invader may well lose.

Of course, civilian defense cannot keep enemy troops from entering the country. But the enemy's entry is an illusion of easy success; it operates as a political ambush. The people will not have allowed themselves to succumb to the psychological condition that Hitler prescribed for successful occupation; they will not have admitted defeat and recognized the occupation regime as their conqueror and master.

Under civilian defense, the country and the defense capacity would not have been defeated. The combat strength would not yet have been applied. The citizenry, trained and prepared, would not feel dismayed or confused. They would understand that the distribution of enemy soldiers and functionaries throughout the country did not mean defeat but instead was the initial stage of a longer struggle at close range. This would be difficult. But the civilian defenders would hold advantages. Set-backs might occur; these could lead, however, to rebuilding strength for future campaigns. There are no white flags of surrender in civilian defense.

Although civilian defense cannot defend the geographic borders, some limited action could be taken even at the *63* initial stage. The deployment of troops could be delayed by obstructionist activities at the docks (if troops came by sea), by refusal to operate the railroads, or by blocking highways and airports with thousands of abandoned automobiles.

Such acts would make clear to the individual enemy soldiers that, whatever they might have been told, they were not welcome as an invasion force. As other symbolic actions the people could wear mourning bands, stay at home, stage a limited general strike, defy curfews, or urge the invading soldiers not to believe their government's propaganda. Such actions would give notice to friend and foe that the occupation will be firmly resisted and at the same time build up the people's morale so as to prevent submission and collaboration.

The invader's parades of troops through the cities would be met by conspicuously empty streets and shuttered windows, and his public receptions would be boycotted. Efforts would be made to undermine the loyalty of his individual soldiers and functionaries. They would be informed that there will be resistance, but that the resistance will be of a special type, directed against the attempt to seize control but without threatening harm to them as individuals. If this could be communicated, the soldiers might be more likely to help the resisting population in small ways, to avoid brutalities, and to mutiny at a crisis point, than they would if they expected at any moment to be killed by snipers or plastic bombs.

Forms of Noncooperation

There would be early forms of more substantial political and economic noncooperation. For example, the invader might meet a blanket refusal by the government bureaucracy and civil servants to carry out his instructions. Or, these officials might continue the old policies, ignore his orders, and disrupt the implementation of new policies. The police might refuse to make political arrests for the invader, warn people of impending arrests, selectively refuse certain orders or carry them out inefficiently.

Attempts to exploit the economic system might be met with limited general strikes, slow-downs, refusal of assistance by or disappearance of indispensable experts, and the selective use of various types of strikes at key points in industries, transportation and the supply of raw materials. News of resistance might be publicized through pre-arranged channels throughout the world, and also be beamed at the invader's homeland. These are only illustrations. Since each case is different, and the enemy's objectives are crucial, obviously there can be no one blueprint for all situations. And it would be important to plan different possible types of strategies for dealing with diverse threats.

Over the long run, both injuries and deaths are to be expected, though they are likely to be much fewer than in military struggles. If the citizens are unwilling to face the prospect of such casualties in their defense action, the resistance will surely collapse; similarly, in a conventional war defeat is certain if the troops when fired upon run the other way or surrender. In this, as in any struggle, casualties must be seen in the context of the campaign as a whole. It is remarkable how many people who accept as natural millions of dead and wounded in a military war find dangers of execution and suffering in civilian defense a decisive disadvantage; this is especially puzzling when there is evidence that casualty rates in nonviolent struggles are vastly smaller than in regular warfare.

Success and Failure

As the occupation develops, the enemy may try to gain control of various institutions, such as the courts, schools, unions, cultural groups, professional societies and the like. If that control is achieved, the future capacity for resistance will be weakened for a long period. Therefore, civilian defense must firmly resist any efforts of the   *65* invader to control the society's institutions. A few examples will show how this could be done.

The courts would declare the invader's bureaucracy an illegal and unconstitutional body; they would continue to operate on the basis of pre-invasion laws and constitutions, and they would refuse to give moral support to the invader, even if they had to close the courts. Attempts to control the schools would be met with refusal to change the school curriculum or to introduce the invader's propaganda, explanations to the pupils of the issues at stake, continuation of regular education as long as possible, and, if necessary, closing the schools and holding private classes in the children's homes.

Efforts to dominate trade unions or professional groups could be met by persistence in abiding by their pre-invasion constitutions and procedures, denial of recognition to new organizations set up by or for the invader, refusal to pay dues or attend meetings of any new pro-invader organizations, and the carrying out of disruptive strikes and economic and political boycotts.

In considering the possibility of failure of civilian defense, or of only very limited success, two factors need to be kept in mind. First, even failure after an heroic struggle by civilian defense would be preferable to any outcome of a major nuclear war. At worst, it would mean a long, difficult and painful existence under severe tyranny, but life would go on, and with life the hope for eventual freedom. Nonviolent action is not a course for cowards. It requires the ability and determination to sustain the battle whatever the price in suffering, yet it would, in the most disastrous case imaginable, still allow a future for mankind. And secondly, in this kind of struggle, failure to achieve total victory would not mean total defeat. Even if the population were unable to drive out the invader, it could maintain a considerable degree of autonomy for the country, and for its institutions upon whose independence any country's freedom largely depends.

The other side of the argument for civilian defense is that under present international and technological conditions this system offers a greater chance of real success in opposing occupation or regaining political freedom than does military defense. When the usurper fails to bring the occupied country to heel, a miasma of uncertainty and dissent would grow within his regime and among his soldiers and officials. International pressures would further weaken the oppressor and strengthen the civilian defenders. Very likely, the usurper would find that he faced not only the opposition of world opinion but significant diplomatic moves and economic embargoes. Continued represion in the occupied country would feed further resistance. The multiplication of noncooperating and disobedient subjects would thus be calculated to defeat the would-be tyrant and bring about a restoration of liberty, enhanced with new meaning, vitality and durability.

The exact way that victory would come would vary from one situation to another. In one case it might coincide with a change of government in the invading country. Or there might be negotiations, with some face-saving formula for the invader. In extremes, the occupation force itself might be so near disintegration and mutiny that with or without such a formula the troops and functionaries would simply go home. In any case, the real meaning would be clear: the occupation would have been defeated.

Another way of looking at civilian defense is to realize that it is *not* disarmament, if disarmament means the reduction or abandonment of defense capacity. Instead, the change-over to civilian defense is *transarmament* — the substitution of a new defense capacity that provides deterrence and defense without conventional and nuclear military power. It also contributes to world peace, since unlike military means civilian defense cannot be used for, or misperceived as intended for, international aggression. *67*

A Policy, Not a Creed

Nor is civilian defense a new doctrine for which unquestioning "believers" are sought. It is a defense policy, not a creed. The stage of development of civilian defense, in theory and practice, is still primitive. Those who have examined the idea differ in their judgments of the types of defense problems, and of enemies, for which it might be suitable. For example, some say it is not possible against a Nazi-type regime, but that it would work against occupation regimes of medium severity. I hasten to add that there is also anything but uniformity of opinion about military defense policies!

Another crucial point about civilian defense is that it is possible for only one or a few countries to adopt the policy initially, without treaties and while most countries remain militarily armed. When convinced of its effectiveness and advantages, other countries too may transarm. Aggressive regimes may well have to be taught lessons concerning the resistance capacity of civilian defense countries.

The first nations to adopt civilian defense are likely to be those that most want self-reliance in defense but which lack the ability to do this with their own military means. The super powers may well follow far behind. It does not, of course, have to be that way, and surprises may occur. A considerable period would doubtless exist in which some countries had transarmed to civilian defense while many others retained military defense — and some of the latter might never change over.

There would inevitably be strongholds of resistance to adoption of this policy. Democratic countries with large military establishments are unlikely, and probably unable, to eliminate these in a short span of time. They might, however, add a civilian defense component, if its effectiveness could be convincingly demonstrated. They might increasingly rely on this component, gradually phasing out the military sector, until the substitution was completed.

Some military personnel could no doubt be retrained to fit into the new civilian defense system.

Dictatorial regimes and unstable governments probably would cling hardest to military capacity for both domestic and international purposes. However, even dictatorships could be influenced toward civilian defense, both by removal of fear of foreign military attack (contributing to internal political relaxation) and by nonviolent pressures for change from their own populations.

It is impossible to predict with certainty the international consequences of the initial cases of transarmament. A nation's decision to adopt a policy of civilian defense and its effectiveness in carrying it out will depend on the state of knowledge of this kind of struggle, the adequacy of the strategic planning, preparations, and training, geographical location, the nature of its enemies, and the determination, skill, and heroism of the people.

Domestic and International Consequences

The successful defeat of a seizure of power or an occupation by a systematic civilian defense policy might make a significant contribution toward the adoption of such a policy by other countries. Initial successes of this policy are likely to lead more and more countries to investigate it and finally to transarm.

Countries that had already adopted civilian defense could directly encourage other nations to transarm. Under "Civilian Defense Mutual Assistance Pacts" several countries could share knowledge, research results, and experience. They could provide certain aid in emergencies (such as food, supplies, finances, diplomatic and economic pressures, a haven for refugees, safe printing and broadcasting facilities). They could give technical advice to countries considering civilian defense, and undertake joint activities to deter aggression by this means.

In contrast with military planning, a sharing of results of civilian defense research, planning and training would not endanger future combat effectiveness. It would instead accelerate the rate at which countries transarmed to civilian defense. This would be of major importance in a step-by-step removal of war from the international scene, and in increasing world security. It is important to note also that even if some countries never abandon military capacity, this would not be a reason for abandoning civilian defense, but rather for expanding it and improving its effectiveness.

Some of the important consequences of civilian defense will be social and economic. For example, transarmament to civilian defense by poor developing countries would probably mean that a large percentage of their present inordinate military budgets could be spent on dealing with poverty and development. Likewise, the developed countries would be able to give more help to the developing world after they convert to civilian defense.

Civilian defense can also deal with domestic or foreign-aided *coups d'état* against the legal government, for which military defense is not designed. (Furthermore, it is usually the military establishment which overthrows the legal government, as in Greece in 1967.)

In the long run, civilian defense would be significantly cheaper than military defense, although it would not be inexpensive. And the transition period, with both military and civilian defense preparations, might be quite expensive.

Another side benefit of civilian defense is that it is likely to make the means of defense serve democratic political ends positively, rather than requiring a foreign policy and alliances that violate a country's avowed democratic principles. No longer would it be necessary in the name of "defense" to make military alliances with dictatorships or to give tacit support to oppressive governments in order to keep military bases. In short, civilian defense would very likely become a potent force around the world for
liberalizing or overthrowing tyrannical regimes.

But most importantly, civilian defense could be expected to restore a very high degree of self-reliance in defense to all countries. It would do this by shifting the source of defense power from modern technology to the people themselves, to their determination and ability to act. If the nations of the world were able, predominantly by their own efforts, and above all without military assistance from the super powers, to defend themselves from internal usurpation by violent minorities and from foreign invasions, the security problems of the world would be altered fundamentally.

The Large Assumption

All of this discussion, of course, is based upon a large assumption: that today's elementary idea of civilian defense can be refined and developed to produce a new kind of defense policy at least as effective as military means. A considerable period of time given over to specific problem-oriented research will be needed to develop the general principles and theoretical frameworks of this policy, to produce models that may lend themselves to adaptation to a particular country's needs, and to complete planning, preparations, training, and other difficult tasks for the transarmament period.

Certainly all would agree that no reasonable possible solution to the problems of modern war and tyranny, and of effective defense against aggression and internal take-overs should be left uninvestigated. It is important now to start the exploration, thought, discussion and research that are needed to make possible a fair evaluation of this concept, and, if it turns out to be workable, to provide the basic knowledge necessary for transarmament, which could be completed within our lifetimes. We are now at a stage in the development of civilian defense at which major advances could be achieved relatively quickly.

Increased confidence in civilian defense and liberation by nonviolent action could produce a chain reaction in the   *71* progressive abolition of both war and tyranny. If this happened, the whole course of history would be altered. Some of the gravest fears and insecurities of the modern world would be lifted. Civilian defense could make it possible to face the future realistically, without fear or panic, but with courage, confidence and hope.

4

Research Areas on Nonviolent Alternatives

INTRODUCTION

Nonviolent action constitutes a large field, the nature of which we know relatively little about. Research on it is urgently needed — whether simply to advance human knowledge, or to provide a basis on which the potentialities, problems, and limitations of nonviolent action as a substitute for violence can be evaluated.

In addition to this "basic" research, problem-oriented investigations are also needed to explore the potentialities and utility of this technique within a country in a variety of conflict situations such as preserving civil liberties, correcting grievances of a minority group, abolishing a dictatorship, or redistributing power and control. Problem-oriented explorations are also needed when this technique is applied to national defense — civilian defense. Here it aims to preserve a society's independence and freedom against both possible internal threats (*coup d'état*) and external threats (invasion) by resistance of the prepared civilian population. Boycotts, strikes, political noncooperation, and defiance are intended not simply to alter the will of the usurper, but to make it impossible for him to establish and to maintain his rule.

Exploration of the potential effectiveness of civilian defense requires a vast amount of research and analysis. These are needed to determine whether or not the assumptions of this policy are valid, and whether the difficult problems involved in its operation can be solved, and if so how. This information would contribute to an improved ability to evaluate the policy of civilian defense as such, and to determine whether or not it merits further attention. If so, such research would help to establish the types of situations and areas in which it may be practicable, if adequately prepared. Further research would also help in deciding the extent to which civilian defense may be suitable in a supplementary capacity, in addition to military defense, and whether civilian defense may provide, as it has been designed, a full effective replacement for military means.

The research areas suggested here are listed without reference to particular academic disciplines. Often a research area or a specific problem may be examined from the perspective of more than one discipline, such as psychology, social psychology, history, political science, and sociology. Some problems, or topics within a problem area, might be explored with aid from the fields of education (especially adult education), anthropology, social ethics, and communications. Scholars in all disciplines are invited to examine these suggested problem areas, and to add to those offered, which are by no means definitive.

The areas for research are grouped here into five broad fields: the technique of nonviolent action itself, internal uses of nonviolent action for nondefense purposes, the nature of threats and conflicts, civilian defense, and implications and consequences of nonviolent alternatives.

Each of the particular areas grouped under these five fields is itself very broad; many individual research topics might be developed under each one. (The bibliography, Chapter 7, indicates existing studies in certain of these areas.)

I. THE TECHNIQUE OF NONVIOLENT ACTION

A. Documentary Studies

1. A Catalog of Cases of Nonviolent Action:

This project would compile as complete a listing as possible of cases of socially or politically significant nonviolent action and of predominantly nonviolent struggles, along with certain standard information about the cases, with bibliographical sources and research clues. Such data as the following might be included: the groups involved, the nature and status of each group; the issue at conflict (specific and general); dates and place of the conflict; motivation for selection of nonviolent behavior; specific methods of action used (as social boycott, civil disobedience, etc.); opponent's methods of repression and/or reaction; results of the struggle. If a typology of nonviolent action conflict situations has by then been developed, the case could be catalogued accordingly. It might be desirable to have a system of cross-filing under the various listed qualities of the struggle to facilitate comparative analyses.

Among the possible uses of such a catalogue are the following:

A. A catalogue of nonviolent cases would make possible the selection of the most relevant cases for study in examining 1) the validity of hypotheses and claims made by proponents and critics concerning the applicability of such methods; 2) the significance of a number of variables operating in nonviolent action as these affect the processes and outcome of the struggle.

B. Such a catalogue would be of considerable assistance in the study of the cultural, political, religious, and other conditions under which this technique has been previously applied.

C. It would provide a means of compiling research clues and bibliographies which may be of considerable assistance later to researchers preparing documentary accounts and analyses of such cases.

The compiling of such material could be divided, roughly, into: 1) historical cases, which would involve library research and consultation with individuals and groups with specialized knowledge; and 2) contemporary cases, involving constant scanning of selected periodicals and communication with persons and groups in various parts of the world who are likely to have such information. This project would be a continuing one, new revisions of the catalogue and new information being issued from time to time.

2. Detailed Multi-factor Computer Catalogue of Cases:

In addition to the research-oriented catalogue of cases, a very different, much more detailed catalogue is needed which would contain information for each case on a large number of standard factors and variables, as complete as possible. This could probably only be done on the basis of detailed case studies as discussed below. This catalogue should be constructed with the use of a computer in mind, which would make the vast amount of material both accessible and manipulable. This would assist in a variety of types of analysis, such as factors which may be common to cases of "success," "failure," and intermediary results. Among the variety of studies which might be made possible with such computer-aided analyses would be the testing of hypotheses by inserting variables into known situations, and constructing situations in order to test hypotheses.

3. Historical Documentary Studies of Cases of Nonviolent Action:

There are far too few detailed documentary accounts of past nonviolent action. Generally speaking there has been little effort to learn from past cases with a view to increasing our general understanding of the nature of this technique, and to gaining particular knowledge which might be useful in future struggles and might contribute to increased substitution of nonviolent action for violence. Study of past cases of nonviolent action and of predominantly nonviolent struggles could provide the basis for a more informed assessment of the future political potentialities of the technique. Detailed documentary accounts can also provide material for analyses of particular facets of the technique and help in the formulation of hypotheses which might be tested in other situations. Preparation of detailed documentary accounts of a large number of specific cases is therefore needed, accompanied if possible by separate collections of existing interpretations and explanations of the events.

From these accounts can be learned, for example, in exactly what kind of situation the technique was used, how it was applied in particular cases, how the actionists and population behaved, how the opponent reacted, what types of repression were imposed, how the actionists and population responded to the repression, how volunteers were obtained, the actionists and population disciplined and organized, and many other aspects.

The accounts need to be as detailed and thorough as is reasonably possible in order to fulfil effectively both the educative function of enabling the reader to learn directly from the past events and also to serve as good bases for analyses and evaluations.

It is important that these studies be as objective as possible, be both intensive and extensive in their coverage, and be written in a factual, descriptive, and readable style. They obviously must be scholarly.

Cases for detailed research may be selected on the basis of such criteria as: 1) the estimated present significance of the case for increasing knowledge, 2) special or unusual characteristics of the case, and 3) the availability of resources, research workers, and historical material. Among the cases which may be particularly relevant are the following: the Russian 1905 Revolution and the February 1917 Revolution; resistance to the 1920 Kapp *Putsch* in Germany; resistance to the 1923 French and Belgian occupation of the Ruhr; the 1930-31 independence campaign in India: Hungarian passive resistance against Austrian rule from 1850-67; the Moslem "Servants of God" nonviolence movement among the Pathans in the North-West Frontier Province of British India, led by Khan Abdul Ghaffar Khan; the defeated 1919-22 Korean symbolic nonviolent protest against Japanese rule; cases where nonviolent action was later abandoned for violence (Nagaland, Tibet, South Africa and others); Latin American nonviolent "civilian insurrections" against dictators (El Salvador and Guatemala in 1944 and Haiti in 1956); the "bloodless revolution" against General Aboud's regime in the Sudan in December 1964 - January 1965; resistance in Nazi-occupied countries during World War II; efforts by noncooperation, obstruction, and demonstrations to save Jews from the Nazi-extermination program; resistance, risings, and revolution in Communist countries (East Germany 1953, Soviet prison camps 1953, Hungary 1956); and Czechoslovak national resistance to invasion and occupation in August 1968. Chapter 7, the bibliography, provides source and reference material on these and other cases.

4. Documentary Studies of Nonviolent Action in American History:

Although obviously not excluded from comprehensive accounts, examples of nonviolent action in American history could be of special interest to American scholars and public, and of importance in possible future practice within this country. Contrary to popular impressions, there exists a vast American history of nonviolent struggles, including colonial struggles before April 1775, international economic sanctions employed by Presidents Jefferson and Madison instead of war, nonviolent abolitionist actions, strikes, economic boycotts by the labor movement, anti-war activities, the civil rights movement, and a large number of others. All of these need to be studied in detail and their roles in United States history evaluated. Revisions may be needed in the overall view of the roles of various types of struggle in the development of the United·States and in assumptions about the necessity of violence in earlier major conflicts.

5. Case Studies of Nonviolent Action — Guerrilla Warfare Mixes:

Several serious strategists have proposed that civilian defense measures would be more effective if combined with guerrilla warfare, terrorism, or other violent resistance. In addition to other projects directly relevant to this problem, it would be of considerable assistance to have case studies of instances in which such a combination happened or was attempted. These would then need to be analyzed in terms of the special ways in which nonviolent action works, and in terms of particular civilian defense problems.

6. Simultaneous Research on Current Struggles:

Also highly important is the preparation of documentary accounts while a nonviolent campaign is proceeding. These may, at times, suffer from unavailability of secret government reports or private records, etc., which might only be available to the public some years or decades later. But this disadvantage would be offset by being able to gather day–by-day detailed information and clues which might otherwise be lost forever. These 79 accounts would be case studies of contemporary social history, drawing upon as much material as possible while the events take place and recording clues to be followed up at a later point. The researchers would thus be producing from original sources data which might otherwise never be recorded; the principal participants would be available for questioning, and the kind of data which has a way of disappearing could be noted. Hypotheses as to the possible course of events and the processes involved could be noted. This phase of study merges into analysis which might or might not be combined with this. In addition to the descriptive accounts, the team of researchers could prepare analyses of the course of events. This type of project for cases of nonviolent action is very similar to that launched several years ago by the Carnegie Endowment for International Peace on instances of interstate conflict.

These on-the-spot research projects depend in part on geographical proximity of current or new cases of nonviolent action, or financial resources, and on the quality and number of research workers available.

B. THE OPERATION OF NONVIOLENT ACTION

7. The Methods of Nonviolent Action:

Further attention is needed to the study of the specific methods or forms of nonviolent action (such as *particular* types of political noncooperation, strikes, boycotts, etc.). Detailed studies are needed of the specific methods and the broad classes of methods, particularly studies using comparative historical material which might shed light on such questions as the conditions in which particular methods may be most applicable and successful, the possible necessity of combining different types of methods, whether the methods used in a given case really influence the power relationships of the contending groups or whether they are largely symbolic and psychological in their impact. These are only illustrative. Further studies might be directed to determining whether deliberate efforts could increase the effectiveness of methods which in the past have not proved outstandingly effective, and to exploring the possible influence on such factors as advance preparations and training. Attention should also be focussed on discovering other methods: existing methods still largely unknown or new methods evolved in the course of actual struggles, or produced by original thought.

8. Dynamics and Mechanisms of Change in Nonviolent Action:

More detailed research is required on the dynamics of the course of struggle in nonviolent action, and to the mechanisms of change which operate in this technique, as distinct from other types of struggle. Case studies are likely to shed light on how these processes and forces operate, and the conditions in which the mechanisms of conversion, accommodation, and nonviolent coercion operate. Various hypotheses on dynamics and mechanisms of this technique are implicit or explicit in the literature. They need to be tested, and new ones developed and subjected also to research. These studies may illuminate the complicated processes of change involved in this type of struggle and the conditions under which successful results are likely.

9. Empirical Research on Current Conflicts:

Various types of polls, questionnaires and interviews may be used to measure responses to nonviolent action in changes in attitudes, opinions, hostility and the like both among the target group and the general public. Such research might be conducted independently of the action group, in cooperation with it, and (rarely) even by the group itself, though problems of bias may then occur. *81*

10. Testing Response to Violent and Nonviolent Behavior:

Psychological experiments and tests, as well as careful examination of past experiences may shed some factual light on the question of the types of responses which may be expected to violence, nonviolent action, and passivity. Various extant assumptions need to be tested, such as the assumption that, when faced with violent behavior only the threat or use of superior violence will halt the original violence ("The only thing they understand is brute force."). Others that need to be tested are: that violent behavior tends to provoke a violent response which tends in turn to provoke further violence; that nonviolent behavior similarly tends to induce in response nonviolent behavior; that repeated nonviolent responses to violence tend to reduce or eliminate the violence; that an absence of strong resistance to aggressive behavior tends to reinforce such aggression and violence. It is desirable to have empirical data on these and comparable assumptions, including the conditions and possible time-lags under which they may operate.

11. Political Power, Its Sources, and Relationship to the Population:

Examination is needed on the nature of political power over large groups of people, its sources, whether (as theorists of nonviolent action maintain) such power depends upon cooperation from the ruled, and whether its withdrawal therefore may threaten the regime. Careful attention is required into such problems as whose cooperation, of what types, and at which times, are most important, and of the roles and limits of repression and other controls for inducing maintenance or resumption of obedience and cooperation.

12. Studies of Violent Struggle:

Not only is it important to understand the nature of violent types of struggle for their own sake, but special studies of such violence are needed to shed light on the ways in which they may both be similar to, and differ from, nonviolent struggle. This general formulation needs to be broken down into specifics. For example, in what ways are guerrilla warfare and nonviolent action similar and dissimilar in their assumptions and dynamics? What can be learned both positively and negatively from studies of military strategy which may be useful in nonviolent strategy? What similar, or (more likely) differing, impacts may violent and nonviolent struggle respectively have on the population and leadership of the opponent group, and also of the struggle group? What similarities and differences may there be in results, short-term and long-term, and side-effects?

The assumptions of the different types of nonviolent action need to be compared with those of different types of violent action, and their respective requirements for effectiveness determined. Specific attention is also needed to the ways in which clashes occur between groups using violent and nonviolent techniques, respectively, and also to the consequences of the introduction of one type of struggle into a conflict predominantly conducted by the other technique.

13. Means and Ends in Struggles:

Efforts are needed to determine how research and critical investigation may be conducted on the possible relationship between the means used in efforts to achieve certain ends, and the ends actually achieved at the conclusion of the effort. What are the relationships between ends and means? Can all, any, or some ends be accomplished by any means? Or, will the use of certain means of action make it impossible to attain the ends which are desired? What are the factors which have in the past produced results which have differed significantly from the goals espoused at the beginning of the struggle? To what degree can a group seeking to produce social change in fact control the outcome? While philosphical analyses are needed in this field, the most important need is to develop concrete measurements and analyses of social causation on these problems.

14. Analyses of the Documentary Studies:

The detailed case studies will make possible a series of individual as well as comparative analyses of these struggles, which may shed important light on the nature of nonviolent action. A large number of specific aspects require attention, either individually or as parts of over-all analyses. The few questions raised here are only illustrative, and many other possible ones may be derived from other sections of this outline of research areas, from study of the literature on the dynamics of this technique, or from independent thought and analysis.

What role may certain underlying conditions play in making possible the use of this technique? What types of individuals tend to use this technique: responsible, alienated, frustrated, altruistic, or other types? What kinds of groups use this technique against what kinds of opponents, and on what types of issues? Are common characteristics between the contending groups required, and, if so, what are they? What are the roles of the nature of the contending groups, their objectives and perceptions of each other? What are the roles and consequences of the means and modes of combat used by the respective groups: for the nonviolent actionists the specific methods applied, and the tactics, strategy, and grand strategy relied upon, possibly with consideration of unused possible alternatives; for the opponent, the means of repression and other counter-measures used, those available to him but not used (and why), and the consequences of his actions, possibly compared with probable consequences of alternative courses of action? How does the nature of the group acting affect the methods, tactics, and strategy used? How does the group's access to certain types of leverage (say, economic) affect the conflict? How can groups with little or no obvious power leverages in the society use non-violent action? How is the struggle affected by extreme objectives of the opponent (religious or political conversion, or extermination)? How, in other ways, do the respective belief systems of the contending groups affect the conflict? How do the relative numbers of the two groups influence the context? What is the role of third parties, does it change and why? To what degree does each side achieve its objectives, or are they denied them? Does a comparative analysis of various cases suggest common factors in successful struggles, in defeats, and in those with mixed results? How does the operation of the dynamics and mechanisms differ from one type of situation to another? What were the key factors, or decisions, or actions which determined the outcome? Are revisions necessary in existing theories and hypotheses? How do longer-term consequences differ from case to case, and why?

15. The Nature and Meaning of Success in Nonviolent Action and Other Techniques:

The varying meanings of the terms "success" and "defeat" need to be distinguished, and consideration given to concrete achievements in particular struggles. This careful examination has rarely been made for violent struggles, the victor and vanquished being assumed to be clear. But if the objectives of each side in the conflict are examined in this context, the matter is much more complex than may at first appear. One or more systems of criteria by which to measure success and defeat in all conflicts, using diverse techniques of action, may therefore be necessary, as well, perhaps, as criteria for such measurement with individual techniques of struggle.

Within the context of civilian defense, as with other defense systems, there appear to be varying degrees of success and defeat which need to be distinguished if the struggles are to be evaluated intelligently and alternative courses of action wisely determined at each stage. A very limited success, for example, if interpreted either as a full success, or as a total failure, may lead to disastrous strategic decisions. For example, failure within a short period of time to get an invader to withdraw fully from an occupied country may nevertheless be accompanied by the frustration of several of the invader's objectives, the maintenance of a considerable degree of autonomy within the occupied country, and the initiation of a variety of changes in the invader's own regime and homeland which may themselves later lead either to the desired full withdrawal, or to further relaxation of occupation rule. With various types of "success" and "defeat" distinguished, it would be highly desirable to have a study of the various conditions under which they have occurred in the past and seem possible in the future. These conditions would include factors in the social and political situation, the nature of the issues in the conflict, the type of opponent and his repression, the type of group using nonviolent action, the type of nonviolent action used (taking into account quality, extent, strategy, tactics, methods, persistence in face of repression, etc.), and, lastly, the possible role and influence of "third parties."

II. INTERNAL USES OF NONVIOLENT ACTION

Most of the history of nonviolent action has been in conflicts within a country, on issues which did not directly involve defense of the legitimate government. Such cases are likely to be important also in the future. While they are not dependent upon adoption of civilian defense, satisfactory experience in their use in place of internal violence — substantiating basic assumptions of the nonviolent technique — would be a contribution to the preparation of the population for civilian defense against more formidable opponents. Conversely, unsatisfactory domestic experience may make people skeptical about more ambitious plans. Many people may be interested in these uses of nonviolent action, though indifferent to the needs and claims for civilian defense.

A large variety of problems are involved within this general field of internal conflict. They have to do not only with the question of how nonviolent action may be used effectively for a variety of particular internal objectives, but also with the relationship of such action to the society as a whole, with the impact on social order and the present or alternate systems of government, with the consequences of the use of these forms of action for objectives which many regard as reactionary and anti-social, and with the broader question of whether or not, in selected area after another, violent sanctions within the society might progressively be replaced with nonviolent ones.

The problems in this area will obviously vary from country to country, and with social, economic and political conditions. A country where a high degree of social justice and democratic controls exist will obviously differ vastly in the roles for nonviolent action from another where a home-grown dictator rules, or where vast inequities in ownership and control of wealth condemn millions to poverty. The intent here is simply to list some of the areas in which investigations are needed of the potential roles and problems of nonviolent alternatives. The problems here are grouped into three broad classes.

16. Protest, Reform and Single Issues:

Nonviolent action may be applied by small or large groups to achieve some limited objective. A particular policy, of a private institution or the government, may arouse dissent and protest which is expressed by use of this technique. Minority and even larger groups, racial, religious, political, sexual, ethnic, and the like may be, or believe themselves to be, discriminated against or denied certain basic liberties which they believe themselves to be entitled to, and hence may resort to nonviolent action to obtain them. Other particular conditions may be seen as injustices to some group; administrative policies and practices may arouse others to act in this manner. In still other cases, people who do not reject military defense as such may use nonviolent action to oppose a particular war and to attempt to bring it to a halt.

17. Alteration of Power Relationships Within the Society:

In other types of situations, nonviolent struggle may be used for producing major alterations of internal power relationships, or even of revolution. The early use by trade unions of strikes and economic boycotts was certainly not simply for economic improvements, but also for changes in the power relationships between private industry and the factory workers; consequently union recognition and political rights, as universal manhood suffrage, were important objectives. Where an internal dictatorship rules, an objective of nonviolent action has on several occassions been its disintegration and destruction. Nonviolent action also has potential which has not been fully developed for altering the ownership and control of aspects of the economy, especially where these are highly concentrated in the hands of a minority of wealthy people while most people live in poverty; land reform, and increased participation in, or transfer of, ownership and control of other aspects of the economy are included here.

18. Maintenance of Order, Liberties, and the Social System

Since nonviolent action may be used to defend, as well as to change conditions, nonviolent action may here be used in various and even conflicting ways. Such methods may be used, for example, against government policies and even against other nonviolent action in order to resist social changes and to prevent progressive improvements in the society. Nonviolent action has also been used to defend the existing social system against efforts of a foreign-aided dictatorial group to remake it according to ideological preconceptions. Attention is also needed to various efforts and proposals deliberately to replace violence with nonviolent action in dealing with various groups within the society (for example the mentally ill, prisoners, juvenile delinquents, suspected criminals); whether nonviolent sanctions might be developed as enforcements of particular laws and practices instead of violence and threats of violence; and how social groups might use nonviolent means of social defense against hostile attacks by other private groups within the society. Examination is also needed of the implications and problems of various groups using nonviolent sanctions against each other in place of either private violence or State violence; would this constitute "creative conflict" or simply produce social disintegration and chaos, leading to greater violence?

Within all three of these areas a large variety of problem-oriented projects can be developed; many other topics are obviously possible. It is important in this area to view such problems from a variety of political perspectives, and to examine the relationship of such direct action to the society itself and the arrangements of its social institutions.

III. THE NATURE OF THREATS FOR WHICH DEFENSE MAY BE NEEDED

19. Examination of the Nature and Needs of Defense:

Before rational examination is possible of the needs of defense and the possible viability of alternative means of meeting those needs, basic re-examination of the meaning of the term "defense" is required. It has come to be used with so many meanings that clarity of thought is impossible until these are separated, and the differing needs, tasks, perceptions, and objectives are distinguished. Attention is also needed to the differing functions which war and other military action have served and do at present, as well as separation of offensive and defensive purposes of military action, and the problems of misperception or misrepresentation concerning these among the civilian population. If defense needs are seen to include both preservation of national independence from foreign attack and occupation and of the legitimate, popularly accepted, regime from minority internal attack and overthrow, then means of effective defense are needed against both foreign and internal attacks – a broader perspective than is common among advocates of military defense.

20. Coup d'état as Internal Usurption:

The large number of cases in which constitutional and other regimes have been overthrown by internal *coup d'état* (with or without foreign support) underlines the importance of defense against such threats and of research attention to the potential role of a civilian defense policy, in defeating them. Past experiences and existing studies of the phenomenon need to be examined with a view to predicting possible lines of action by such a usurping group, the vulnerable points and periods in such *coups*, the types of forces and conditions which may weaken or strengthen resistance to such an internal attack, and various possible strategies which might be employed against internal usurpation. Attention would also be required to the possibilities of new types of *coups* which might arise in countries with civilian defense policies, such as a *coup* in the change-over period by supporters of military defense, or actions attempted later by tiny fanatical groups which might estimate the country to be vulnerable even to them.

21. Gradual Erosion or Abdication of Constitutional Government:

The established constitutional system is sometimes destroyed gradually or officially, rather than by a quick stroke, as in a *coup*. Increasing suppression of civil liberties, growth of police and administrative powers, reduced effective legislative controls over the executive, by-passing or suspension of constitutional provisions, and even direct surrender by the legislature of its powers to the executive — as in the Enabling Act in Germany in 1933 — are illustrations of stages in which a phased destruction of constitutional government occurs. Attention is vitally needed also to the social conditions under which these changes occur and are accepted by the populace, such as a growth of internal violence and chaos within the country perhaps combined with international crises. Clearly at such times if the constitutional system is to be defended it requires support from the citizenry. Work is therefore needed to shed light on the conditions in which this threat occurs and is successful, and to the means of civilian defense of the constitutional system which may then be effectively applied.

22. Guerrilla Warfare as Usurpation:

Examination is needed as to 1) whether a country with a prepared civilian defense policy would be vulnerable to attempted minority usurpation in the form of guerrilla warfare or related terrorization of the population intended to produce noncooperation with, and the collapse of, the legitimate government; and 2) if so, what types of nonviolent strategies, tactics, and methods might be most appropriate in meeting such attempted guerrilla usurpation. Further, study would be needed to examine whether in the absence of advance preparations a country already under guerrilla attack could, by civilian defense measures, defeat the guerrillas by noncooperation and refusal to become terrorized into submission.

91

23. Blockades as Limited Foreign Attack:

Certain countries or other political units are, because of their geography, size, and economy, especially vulnerable to external pressures by land, sea, or air blockades, or a combination of them. Britain and West Berlin are two obvious examples, but there are many others. If a hostile foreign regime were successfully deterred from military invasion by the civilian defense country's resistance capacity, the frustrated regime might seek to use its military forces to make the threatened country surrender or grant certain demands by imposing a blockade. This would be especially serious when it could drastically affect the supply of food and the economy. Or blockades might be imposed in quite different contexts, as the famous Berlin Blockade. The question then arises whether, and if so how, measures compatible with civilian defense could be used to break the blockade, and what within the blockaded country might be done to help it withstand the pressures. The Berlin experience and the successful airlift of food without military exchanges would be a case for study, but attention would be needed to quite different situations and varying types of blockades.

24. Invasions:

Conventional military invasions still occur, sometimes alone, and sometimes combined with another type of usurpation or attack, such as a foreign-supported *coup*. Conventional military defense forces are primarily designed to deal with foreign invasions; indeed, this capacity has historically been their final justification. It is for this type of attack that civilian defense was originally primarily developed, and for which it remains especially suitable. Research is needed in the varying forms which invasions may take, and the differing objectives for which they may be launched. These are highly important in formulating effective civilian defense measures, for the resistance should be able to thwart his objectives.

Although minor delaying actions against the incursions of foreign troops and functionaries may be possible, civilian defense for various reasons does not attempt to halt such entry, and cannot successfully do so; the emphasis instead is on making the populace ungovernable by the foreign invaders. Problems of perception of intention and capacity therefore exist for everyone concerned, and research on them is needed. Diverse other research problems concerning invasions may arise, including the previous relationships between the countries, the balances of populations, economic power and the like, political outlooks and ideologies of the countries, differences where there is more than one invader, particular problems where the objective is highly limited, in contrast to complete reconstruction of the society of the invaded country and ideological conversion of its population. These are simply illustrative of the many specific topics requiring attention within this area.

25. Bombings of Civilian Defense Countries:

There are conflicting opinions on the possibility that countries adopting civilian defense would be bombed. According to one view, a foreign enemy recognizing the immense problems of ruling a country with civilian defense might simply seek to impose its will on the country or remove this peculiar type of threat by destroying its cities or other important points with conventional or nuclear bombs, either on a progressive or periodic basis, or in one all-out attack. Proponents of the opposite view hold that there would be virtually no possibility at least of a nuclear attack against a country which had neither nuclear nor conventional military capacities. Between the extremes there are those who feel that, under certain conditions at least, such bombings might well take place, and that hence civilian defense presumes pre-nuclear World War II conditions and has no relevance in today's world. In any case, a variety of strategic military and political factors would be involved for the attacking country. For the country with civilian defense, several research problems invite attention, including examination of measures which could reduce the chances of attack, alternative responses to threatened nuclear blackmail, methods of encouraging internal rebellion against the threatening regime at home, and ways to carry on if bombing threats were carried out. Examination is also required of the validity of the various views on the possibility of bombings under these conditions.

26. Cultural Survival and Foreign Rule:

There have been a number of instances in which extended foreign occupation and rule has resulted in one of two extremes: the elimination of an identifiable distinct culture of the conquered population; or the survival of the culture in face of these conditions for hundreds of years. What are the important causal factors which facilitate or prevent cultural survival, the roles of linguistic, religious, cultural, and social factors in this phenomenon? Individual and comparative studies of such cases might shed important light on the conditions under which it is possible for a people to preserve its way of life under the most adverse conditions.

27. Occupation Policies and Measures:

It would be foolhardy to concentrate all research attention on possible actions of the civilian defenders. One must focus attention also on the types of occupation policies and measures which have been used in the past by international aggressors and empires in efforts to subdue and rule the conquered territories and their populaces. Particular attention should be directed to recent developments, some possible innovations in such policies and measures, and to possible future developments. These studies will provide suggestive insights into the kinds of situations and measures which the civilian defenders may have to face.

28. Repression and Other Counteraction Against Nonviolent Struggle:

The enforcement problems against a group or population using nonviolent means of struggle are quite distinct from those arising in cases of general lawlessness or from some type of violent struggle. Experience has gradually begun to accumulate as a result of governmental, police, and military counter-measures; and it is certain that a group or regime seriously contemplating military usurpation against a civilian defense country would try not only to review this experience but also to devise innovations. It is therefore highly important that the civilian defenders themselves should be aware of these in some detail in order to be able to meet such measures and to prepare possible countering responses.

29. The Nature and Weaknesses of Totalitarian and Other Dictatorships:

Resistance to a possible dictatorial enemy requires that the enemy must be known well, not only in terms of his ideology, objectives, and obvious strengths, but in terms of his inadequacies, weaknesses, vulnerable points and the like, in short, his Achilles' heels. There is much evidence that extreme dictatorships are often much weaker and more fragile than they are believed to be. Knowledge of these general features and specific characteristics of a particular system may be highly important in determining the appropriate strategy for resisting and undermining it.

IV. CIVILIAN DEFENSE: PROBLEMS OF ADOPTION, POLITICS AND PRACTICE

A. Adoption and Basic Operation

30. Conceptions of Nonviolent Action in American Society:

If one is considering the possibility of trying to convince Americans that nonviolent action is a practical alternative to violence, or that a civilian defense policy could be a practical substitute for military defense, one would need to know more about present American views of these phenomena:

1) How do Americans conceive of nonviolent action? What is the extent of their knowledge and understanding? What do they think of when they hear or read the words "nonviolent resistance", "passive resistance", " nonviolent action", Gandhi, Martin Luther King, etc.?

2) What arguments do they offer in favor of the technique and against it?

3) Is there any conception at all, and if so what type, of the possibility of resisting by popular action a foreign occupation or attempted internal take-over?

4) Is there any more, or less, evidence of understanding of the phenomena themselves if differing terminologies are utilized in the investigations?

The second and third parts of this would require more than simply answering straight questions, the answers to which might be superficial or even inaccurate representations of the real attitude; depth interviews or some similar method would probably be required. It would be important to search for both "intellectual" and "emotional" reasons, as those possibly associated with sex roles. It is possible, but not certain, that these two objectives might be realizable with the same project. It would seem important that answers be sought to these questions among various sections of the populace to find out, for example, what differences may exist between intellectuals and nonintellectuals, Negroes and non-Negroes, urban and rural people, upper, middle, and lower classes, various broad religious groups and possibly parts of the country. Careful control of the samples chosen would be essential.

One or more pilot experiments might be provided to follow up the major studies in which given previously interviewed subjects would be subjected to attempts to provide them with information attempting to answer their main objections or correct their misconceptions. They would then, after a time lapse, be interviewed again to determine what, if any, effect the effort had made. A control group would, of course, be necessary for effective validation of this study.

31. Achieving Understanding and Acceptance of Civilian Defense:

Even if one assumes that the many practical problems involved in making civilian defense sufficiently effective to merit adoption in place of military defense, there remain a variety of obstacles to its acceptance among the general population; without such acceptance it could never work. Attention is therefore needed to the problems of overcoming both irrational and rational obstacles to it. Some of these are related to the problems discussed in the previous section, but others have to do entirely with civilian defense. In what ways can the assumed identification of defense with violence be altered? How can the historical distortions concerning the roles of violent and nonviolent action be corrected? Under what conditions will people be willing to participate in their own defense instead of leaving the matter to experts and professionals? How will a transition period, in which military defense will be phased down and eventually out only as civilian defense measures are well prepared, affect people's attitudes? What role is there for the assumed psychological propensity to violence? What relevant to adoption of civilian defense can be learned from past cases where people who normally had accepted military means have, for limited periods, used unprepared nonviolent resistance for national defense purposes? How do perceptions of nuclear weapons as deterrents affect possible attitudes to adoption of civilian defense? Are there psychological blocks to acceptance of a deterrence capacity by civilian defense preparations? These are only illustrative. Also important are questions of educational and political strategy for gaining acceptance and adoption of civilian defense.

32. Political Factors in Civilian Defense:

As civilian defense is much more intimately associated with the political conditions of the defending country than is military defense, serious attention is required to what political conditions may be required for, or most suitable for, effective civilian defensive measures. Various questions arise here, of which these are only suggestive. Is there a minimal degree of popular participation in government required for this policy? Is a considerable degree of political decentralization required or not? Is a particular degree of formal political education among the population required? Can civilian defense be adapted for newly-independent countries? What are the differences in the conditions for the operation of the defense policy between various types of countries (thinly and densely populated, large, medium, and small, various types of terrain and climates)? Could civilian defense make possible greater degrees of democracy within the country itself? What of the possible role of either indirect influences or direct efforts to encourage the liberalization or disintegration of dictatorial foreign and domestic regimes as a contribution to reduced incidence of international conflict and aggression? Is there an intrinsic connection between democratic political systems and the requirements for popular participation in civilian defense struggle, or not?

33. The Change-over Period, Training and Preparations:

The transarmament to civilian defense would require not only vast advance research and planning, but immense programs of training the population in how to conduct such resistance and otherwise preparing for these eventualities. These other preparations might include a large variety of steps, such as provision of material supplies, means of communication, food supplies, etc. In addition, there would be a difficult transition period of some years between full dependence on military defense and full dependence on civilian defense while these preparations and training were being carried out and the country was increasing its civilian "combat strength" to the point where it was felt possible to abandon the military element. These extraordinarily complex problems require very careful and full examination.

34. Forms for Resistance Organizations:

Under conditions of severe repression and dictatorial or totalitarian controls the problems of operating an organized resistance movement become serious. That organized resistance has happened in the past, however, proves that these obstacles are not insuperable, although they do require both research into how these were dealt with in past cases and examination of possible innovations which might be of use in future emergencies. In addition to problems of structure and day-to-day communication within the movement and with the general population, attention will be needed to the degree to which the actual organization can or cannot be set up in advance of the usurpation and the degree to which unstructured or spontaneous mass actions may play a role. (In the latter actions, the population would act on the basis of pre-determined plans which would operate in the case of given anticipated events even if a separate resistance organization were unable to act because of arrests etc.) Various other factors in relation to organization need examination, including the roles of neighborhood and occupational groupings, religious and political bodies, i.e., the normal institutional structure of the society.

35. Strategy and Tactics of Civilian Defense:

The field of strategy and tactics in civilian defense is at least as complex as in conventional military defense, and may be even more so, as the combatants are likely to *99* consist of nearly the full population of the transarmed country and virtually all of the organizations and institutions of that country are likely to be involved. Attention will be needed, first, to general principles of strategy and tactics in nonviolent action as a political technique of struggle; this will require examination of past strategies and tactics. Possible innovations in general types may be considered in light of the dynamics and mechanisms of nonviolent action.

But in addition to such general principles, attention will be needed to possible alternative strategies and tactics to meet a large variety of specific types of situations, as influenced by such factors as the country or part of the country threatened, the nature of the internal or foreign usurper (including his ideology, sources of power, means of repression and other influence), the objectives of the opponent, and his possible strategies and tactics. It would be important to work out systematically a considerable variety of strategic and tactical responses to various kinds and stages of attack as well as to develop the stages and measures by which one goes from strictly defensive action to offensive action in an attempt to disintegrate the usurper's power and regime.

36. Special Questions of Methods and Tactics:

Certain special problems in the waging of civilian defense struggles may require particular attention. The following are simply suggestive: What are the forms and effects, respectively, of full or selective social boycott, and of fraternization and other types of contact (without collaboration) with the personnel of the occupying forces? What role should the legitimate police play in resistance against an occupation or internal take-over? For example, should they resign, disappear, continue the legal duties but refuse illegitimate orders, pretend to collaborate but be inefficient (lose records, warn persons to escape before

attempting arrests, be unable to locate wanted persons,

etc.), seek to arrest individuals of the occupation force or usurping regime? What capacity do armed forces and police units have for disciplined nonviolent action? This might be important in two types of situations: first, if civilian defense were initially adopted by a country for the limited purpose of dealing with a *coup d'état*, and second, if it were deemed desirable to keep together existing disciplined groups and teams, giving them new tasks for carrying out security duties. What should civil servants do in particular types of crises? Should they strike, engage in selective noncooperation, carry out legitimate policies only and "work-on," "lose" key records, etc.? If enemy armed forces occupy the capital, should the main governmental officials flee and maintain a new headquarters elsewhere in the country or abroad, or should they try to continue to carry out legitimate duties until arrested, or go underground as a basis for resistance and a parallel government in the country itself, or some combination of these, with perhaps different persons assigned to different roles? What is to be learned from past experience with parallel government which is relevant to civilian defense? What is the contribution of international economic sanctions against aggressors or usurpers generally, and especially in relation to support for attacked civilian defense countries? What is to be learned, positively or negatively, from past international attempts at economic boycotts and embargoes, as against Mussolini's Italy, South Africa, and Rhodesia, and what are the conditions which must be met if they are to be most effective?

B. Special Problems

37. Possible Combination of Civilian Defense with Military Defense, Guerrilla Warfare and Sabotage:

While most exponents of civilian defense have recognized the inevitability of a period of transition in which civilian defense preparations and military defense preparations would co-exist, considerable disagreement exists relative to the advisability of using such a combination in a permanent policy. On the one hand, some have advocated combining civilian defense with conventional military defense, so that the former would go into operation after the failure of the latter; others have advocated abandoning of frontal military defense measures, but combining civilian defense with guerrilla warfare and/or sabotage measures, with different tasks being assigned to the different types of struggle. On the other hand, some theorists argue that although it seems immediately appealing to use all possible types of struggle in the attempt to get the maximum total combat strength, the problem of the "mix" is not that simple. Instead, they contend, such a combination may destroy some highly important strategic advantages of civilian defense alone, and because the techniques possess quite different mechanisms and dynamics, the use of violent means may seriously interfere with or destroy the power-altering capacities of civilian defense. For example, it may be part of a strategy of a civilian defense struggle to seek to obtain the mutiny of the enemy's soldiers, or at least attain sufficient uncertainty or sympathy from them that they are deliberately inefficient in obeying orders; but if they and their friends are being shot at or killed, this possibility is enormously reduced. Because of the complexity of the problem of "the mix," it requires serious research and analysis.

38. Cases of Little or No Dependence on the Population: In most types of usurpation, there is a considerable degree of dependence on the population of the country which has been seized, and hence a strong basis for opposition by noncooperation. However, in certain unusual types of aggression this is not the case; if civilian defense measures are to operate at all in such cases, they must do so by quite different means. These situations are illustrated by military occupation of unpopulated mountainous or desert areas for such purposes as military bases, transportation or communications purposes, or international psychological effects; the seizure of a limited coastal area or port as a naval base (such as Gibraltar) without other attempt to control the country as a whole; or cases in which an invader would intend to deport or annihilate the entire original population and replace them by his own colonists.

39. Technological Developments and Civilian Defense:

Modern developments in the technology of communication, transportation, police methods, as well as psychological manipulation, pose serious problems for civilian defense. Opposing views have been presented concerning these. Rapid communication and transportation clearly make it easier for a usurper to move against centers of resistance, but can technological developments also be used to assist the resisters? Transistorized broadcasting sets and radios are one small example. Are the influences of technological and scientific developments altered in any way by the type of nonviolent resistance used: whether it operates with complete openness and defiance; whether it attempts to operate on the basis of secrecy for a major part of its activities; whether a small group aims to remain in hiding directing operations; or whether the whole population knows what to do in various contingencies without further instructions, and the like? Investigation of these and many other problems is needed by people familiar with both civilian defense and communication developments.

40. The Roles of Economic Organization and Industrial Technology:

Production and distribution systems are important in the conduct of civilian defense and for most rulers or occupation regimes. But since the social organization and   *103* the technology for these systems can differ so widely, these differences may produce diverse problems for civilian defense. Even for centralized industrial systems, opposite conclusions have been reached by those who have considered the problem; these conclusions range from the view that extreme agrarian decentralization is necessary for effective resistance, to the position that resistance is more effective in a centralized industrial system, since highly vulnerable key points may cause selective noncooperation to disrupt the whole system. Complex problems also relate to the degree of national self-sufficiency of the economy versus international economic interdependence. Automation introduces new factors into an already difficult problem area. Examination should also be made of types of economic noncooperation which might be most suitable against usurpers with a variety of political and economic objectives.

41. Riots in Civilian Defense Countries:

Riots within a civilian defense country are possible under such conditions as the following: the existence of deep divisions within the country on political, economic, cultural, linguistic, or racial lines; the existence of a strong group intent on using violent means to obtain a restoration of military defense; the presence of a significant number of sympathizers with a hostile foreign power; widespread boredom among youths seeking excitement in nonpolitical rioting. Various investigations of such rioting are required in relation to civilian defense; for example: determining effects of such rioting on civilian defense capacity; whether, and if so how, civilian defense preparations might include measures to reduce or prevent rioting; the nature and workings of both nonlethal and nonviolent means of controlling large crowds and halting rioting; examination of existing experience in the use of police and military means of riot control, and the relationship of such means to other factors.

C. Civilian Defense for Particular Countries

42. Pilot Feasibility Studies:

Several pilot projects should be undertaken to examine the feasibility of civilian defense in specific situations of relatively limited scope, against a particular type of threat. Such studies would involve extensive information about the assumed attacker, the defending country, and the international situation. It would be important to know the attacker's objectives, ideology, probable strategies and methods, international position, degree of internal stability and support, and possible explanations or justifications for his attempted usurpation. Knowledge required about the defending country or area would include: the social structure, political system and traditions; intensity of commitment to the society and principles being defended, the state and vitality of the economy, structure, composition and degree of dependence on external markets or supplies; the degree and type of presumed advance training for civilian defense and experience with nonviolent action; the communication and transportation systems; geographical characteristics; general and particular characteristics of population; and the like. Relevant international factors include: the degree of dependence of the usurper on other countries; the type, intensity and distribution of sympathies and attitudes throughout the world toward the defenders and usurpers; and the existence or absence of advance agreements and preparations for other countries and international bodies to offer various types of concrete assistance in such situations. Determination of specific forms of possible international assistance would also be important. These might include supplies, food, monetary aid, radio, printing, diplomatic assistance, economic sanctions against the usurper, refusal of recognition of the usurper and/or expulsion of his regime from international organizations, etc.

With this basic information, very concrete plans would need to be drawn up to meet the presumed usurpation, each considering possible alternative strategies and methods of resistance which might be most appropriate, in view of the factors previously examined the opponent's possible and probable types of reaction and repression along with the means of countering these, the roles of resistance by the general population, as well as by specific occupational, age, or geographical groups and other specific factors.

Such pilot feasibility studies might be worked out to meet such situations as the following:

1) The defense of West Berlin against an attempted East German or Soviet military take-over.

2) The defense of Norway against a conventional military attack and occupation, either by the Soviet Union or by some other power.

3) The defense of Poland against a revanchist German attack.

4) The defense of civilian constitutional government against military or other *coups d'état* in Zambia, Tanzania, the Dominican Republic, Italy, or the United States.

5) Resistance to attempts to impose minority one-party dictatorships by guerrilla warfare, as in Thailand or Burma, including economic and political factors and specific means of noncooperation and refusal to submit to terrorism.

6) Defense by a small Latin American country against U.S. political and military intervention in its internal affairs.

43. Civilian Defense and Disengagement in Central Europe:
Proposals for various types of disengagement in Central Europe to reduce East-West tension all have to face the question of how such countries would be expected to defend themselves, once American or Russian troops had been withdrawn, in case of foreign invasion or attempted minority take-overs, without setting off a major East-West war in the process. The existence of a self-reliant, effective defense capacity in Central Europe could facilitate a

pulling back by both Russian and American armed forces, because their presence is now supported by fear. In non-Communist countries of the area, the fear is that without such forces they would be subject to Communist invasion or take-over; and in East European countries it is that without Russian forces they might again be victims of neo-Nazi German aggression. The possibilities of civilian defense would need to be examined and developed for specific cases, and its potentialities and problems would need to be compared with those of alternative defense policies, whether conventional military, paramilitary, or some combination of one or both of these (and their subtypes).

44. Civilian Defense for the United States?

While most analysts expect that civilian defense will first be adopted by such small countries as Sweden, Norway, or Denmark, and that military Super Powers, such as the United States or the Soviet Union, are likely to be last, various projects are needed on the relevance and possibilities of civilian defense for the U.S. and other large countries.

Analysis would be needed of the variety of defense and military-related needs, present, unacknowledged, and future. Not only would obvious differences between defense and offense capacity need analysis and separation, but also separation of the defense of the United States itself from defense measures for other countries. Exploration of the possible role of civilian defense in making smaller countries self-sufficient in defense capacity, when they are unable to achieve that by military means is needed; U.S. aid in know-how on civilian defense for those countries should be explored. What would be the impact on U.S. defense and military needs if self-defense capacity were restored to all countries which might be threatened by domestic usurpation or foreign invasion?

What would be the defense needs of the United States itself, and to what degree could civilian defense meet them? What about the claims that much of U.S. military capacity exists not to defend the country and people, but to defend overseas imperialist economic interests and to support and extend power interests of the U.S. government in diverse parts of the world? What validity is in those charges? How does this affect civilian defense, which has a more limited, defensive, capacity? If the charges be true, what would be the impact on present policies if the citizenry became convinced that civilian defense was effective for genuine defense needs of the United States itself?

How can the special problems of nuclear weapons be handled, and how would this affect the program for the transarmament (change-over) period. Are large countries, such as the U.S., easier or more difficult than small ones to defend by this civilian policy? What types of internal defense needs would Americans need to prepare to meet? What economic programs might be required for the phasing out of war industry, for job re-training, for new domestic or overseas programs that might accompany or follow adoption of civilian defense? Again, these are only illustrative of the many problems requiring examination.

V. IMPLICATIONS AND CONSEQUENCES OF NONVIOLENT ALTERNATIVES

45. Domestic Consequences:

Since civilian defense constitutes a direct defense of the society by action of the civilian population and their organizations and institutions, it is very possible that this policy has implications for changes in the society. (Since military defense also seems to have rather different, largely centralizing, influences on the society, there should not be a surprise that this alternate policy may also have certain influences.) The extent and nature of these social consequences require attention. Are they simply decentralization and vitalization of participation in the institutions of the society, or are there other less obvious consequences likely, either good or bad? Are structural changes required or not? What kinds of society can be defended by civilian defense, and how — with difficulty, with ease, or not at all? This needs to be examined on the basis of historical evidence, not ideological preconceptions. Do efforts to improve the society become, simultaneously then, defense efforts? What are the likely effects on the society of civilian defense, in terms of possible increased politicization, and training of the citizenry in methods of non-violent action?

46. Civilian Defense and Foreign Policy:

Under present conditions, as in the past, foreign policy and military defense are usually seen as inter-related, and often highly so. Probably a much closer relationship would exist between civilian defense measures and the country's foreign policy. Measures to reduce the prospects of international aggression, to resist the rise and continuation of dictatorships, to gain friends abroad (even within possible enemy countries), and to expand the number of countries relying on civilian defense policies, possibly with mutual aid of various types among them, etc. would all require careful advance and continual attention.

47. Civilian Defense and National and International Law:

Civilian defense would require a number of changes in the laws of a nation adopting it. These would include not only the acts authorizing its adoption for defense of the country and particular ways for handling the change-over period, but also a whole series of other legal measures, including authorization for various types of preparations, training, research establishments, planning agencies, defense organizations and institutions. Legislation might *109* also be appropriate to deal with the obligation of citizens to participate in training for civilian defense, and to defend the country in times of crisis, potentially including certain standards and some type of sanctions against collaboration. In a large country, and especially in a federal system such as the United States, various types of state, provincial, or local legislation would also probably be required.

It is possible that a reformulation or refinement of certain standards of international law might be needed, especially concerning the rights and duties of citizens of occupied countries, the duties of other governments in their relations with an aggressor country, and their duties vis-a-vis the legitimate constitutional government and population of the country which is the victim of international aggression or of internal minority usurpation. These are simply illustrative of legal questions requiring attention.

48. International Reactions to the Limited Adoption of Civilian Defense:

Attention is needed to the various possible international consequences of the adoption of civilian defense by only one or a few countries, while others maintained their military capacities. One may hypothesize reactions from one extreme to the other from invasion by an expansive military power regarding this as an invitation to aggression, to the inducement of a rival power, no longer fearing attack, to transarm similarly to civilian defense. The real situation, however, would be at best much more complicated than this implies. It is important to weigh the possibilities of such reactions in order to explore preparations for meeting them; this will also assist in evaluations of the policy itself.

49. Self-liberation of Countries Already Under Tyrannical Rule:

The use of nonviolent struggle in countries already

under a domestic or foreign dictatorship does not formally come under "civilian defense" which implies *advance* preparations and training in peacetime to meet attempted usurpations. Such self-liberation is, however, related to the defense policy in a number of ways.

1) The chances of international aggression may diminish as a result of the alteration or overthrow of expansionist dictatorships.

2) Military aggression by such a regime against a country with a civilian defense policy may, under certain circumstances (according to some exponents of civilian defense) lead to a rising in the invader's homeland.

3) In peacetime preparations in civilian defense countries might stimulate liberation groups to apply similar methods and related strategies against their own internal oppressive regime. All these, and many other related possibilities, and the numerous problems they involve, would require considerable research and analysis.

50. Consequences of Civilian Defense Capacity for International Relations:

Examination needs to be given to at least three aspects of this area. First the development of a country's internal capacity for this type of self-defense may contribute to altering past relationships and forming new ones with a particular country (or countries) which has in the past exercised some form of dominance – even outright occupation – over it. The beginnings of a change in the relationship may rest in large degree on a recognition by the formerly dominant country that the use or threat of military power is no longer capable of achieving domination, and on a recognition by the formerly subordinate country that its self-reliance is basically dependent on nonmilitary factors. The alteration of the relationship between Norway and Sweden (the turning point being the crisis of 1905) may be an instructive case. Today, despite some feelings of hostility, recourse to violence between the countries is virtually inconceivable. Altered relationships between certain ex-colonial powers and their former colonies may also provide insights. In addition to the specific role of capacity for effective struggle, associated social and economic conditions would probably merit attention.

Second, attention should be given to the kind of international relationships which might exist in a world in which one, several, or even many countries had transarmed to civilian defense while others maintained their conventional military or nuclear capacities. This problem requires not only speculation but careful examination of the variety of influences and forces which might be operative under diverse circumstances.

Third, examination should be made of the possible forms which international relationships and international organizations might take in a world in which many or most countries had transarmed to civilian defense. Such an international system would obviously differ not only from that of today, but also from a world government with a monopoly of military power. What would be its characteristics? What are the forms of concerted international action most appropriate for dealing with aggressive military-armed countries, who are either fighting each other or are attacking countries with civilian defense policies?

51. The United Nations and Civilian Defense:

There are a whole series of possible roles related to civilian defense for various branches and agencies of the United Nations and other international organizations. The following are simply suggestive: research and dissemination of information about this defense policy to member countries; international inspection of transarmed civilian defense countries to ensure to others that the change-over is genuine; investigation and dissemination of facts when international aggression takes place; condemnation of the aggressor before world opinion; the institution of various types of international political and economic sanctions against the aggressor; the launching of various types of help to the attacked civilian defense country (such as monetary aid, supplies, broadcasting facilities, continued recognition only of its legitimate government, etc.); and possible action by certain types of U.N. forces intervening in the situation.

It is also possible that the United Nations might play a role if civilian defense were adopted simultaneously by several countries in a coordinated and phased program of transarmament, say, on a continental basis or as a part of a program of tension-reduction and demilitarization in certain areas. Various other roles might exist for the United Nations in relation to civilian defense. But any effective U.N. support would require advance examination and planning. The research possibilities are numerous.

5

85 Cases of Nonviolent Action

The survey in Chapters 1 and 2 of the historical development of nonviolent action as a political technique does not convey the extent and significance of its past application. The simple list of 85 cases which is offered in this chapter may be useful until further research can take place. It provides at least a glimpse of the past scope of nonviolent action. Together with other examples in the text, it provides a basis for suggesting that certain popular conceptions about nonviolent action are not true. The very considerable differences among these listed struggles, as to types of issues, groups involved, countries in which they took place, historical and cultural backgrounds, etc., should be noted. Although the list cannot be representative, it is possible to draw a few very tentative impressions, which is done at the end of this appendix.

Among the other variations in the cases here are the number of participants, the degree of conscious rejection of violence, the relative importance of a distinguishable leadership, the type of opponent faced, the amount of repression applied, and the objectives sought.

After each item there is an indication of the nature of the group applying the technique. In two cases the action was taken by a single individual, Gandhi, but had a major social and political effect. These cases are indicated by *IND*. In five cases action was wholly or partly taken by small, highly committed groups, usually of less than fifty persons. These cases are indicated by *SM*. In the vast majority of cases, however, the action was taken by a large group, from fifty to many thousands of people. These cases are indicated by *LG*. These three classes were all characterized by reliance on nonviolent action (whether deliberate or accidental, principled or expedient) as a part of what might be called a "grand strategy": the substitution of nonviolent action for violent conflict was almost or fully complete.

There remains, however, a small group of seven or eight cases in which the substitution of nonviolent for violent conflict was not complete, and violence was also used. In these cases – the Norwegian and Danish resistance during the Nazi occupation, for instance, and the Hungarian Revolution – violence was not excluded on the basis of either principle or "grand strategy," and violent methods were used to a significant extent. However, in these cases nonviolent action was also used to a significant extent, i.e., at least fifty percent of the total "combat strength," or of the combination of all means of sanctions applied. These cases involved the use of nonviolent means of active struggle, such as strikes and noncooperation. During particular phases nonviolent action was used almost exclusively, as, for example, in the resistance of the teachers and clergy in Norway, or the general strikes in Copenhagen and Amsterdam. Had such nonviolent means not been used in these cases, there might have been a

relatively greater application of violent methods of

conflict, or a reduction of the total "combat strength". These cases are indicated by *MX*.

The 85 cases are classified under headings indicating the type of grievance felt by the group using nonviolent action. In several cases there is an overlap and a given case might therefore be listed under more than one heading.

A. Against Oppression of Minorities:
1. Civil resistance struggles by Indian minority in South Africa, 1906-14 and 1946. *LG*
2. Vykom temple road satyagraha (India), 1924-25. *SM*
3. Various campaigns in U.S. civil rights movement, especially from 1955, such as Montgomery, Alabama, Negro bus boycott, 1955-56; Tallahassee, Florida, Negro bus boycott, 1956; sit-ins and freedom rides, 1961-62; the 1963 march on Washington, D.C.; and other cases. *LG*
4. Civil resistance by Tamils in Ceylon, 1956-57, and 1961. *LG*

B. Against Exploitation and Other Economic Grievances:
1. Mysore (India) noncooperation, 1830. *LG*
2. Irish rent strike and tax refusal, 1879-86. *MX*
3. Boycott of Captain Boycott by Irish peasants, 1880. *LG*
4. Buck's Stove and Range boycott (U.S.), 1907. *LG*
5. British general strike, 1926. *LG*
6. U.S. sit-down strikes, 1936-37. *LG*
7. French sit-down strikes, 1936-37. *LG*
8. "Reverse strikes," various cases in Italy, at least since 1950, including mass fast and reverse strike in Sicily led by Danilo Dolci, 1956. *LG*
9. General strike in Gambia, January 1961. *LG*
10. Spanish workers' strikes in the Asturias mines and elsewhere, 1962. *LG*
11. Delano grape workers strike in California, and national and international boycott of grapes 1965-70. *LG*

(Many other cases of strikes and boycotts could be included here, and would greatly add to the number of cases of the use of the technique in the West. Noncooperation in the form of strikes and, to a lesser extent, economic boycotts, has been the main weapon of industrial workers and trade unionists.)

C. Against Communal Disorders:
1. Gandhi's fast in Calcutta, 1947. *IND*
2. Gandhi's fast in Delhi, 1948. *IND*

D. On Religious Issues:
1. Early Christians' reaction to Roman persecution. *LG*
2. Early Quakers' resistance to persecution in England, late seventeenth century. *LG*
3. Roman Catholic struggle vs. Prussian Government over mixed marriages, 1836-40. *LG*
4. Roman Catholic resistance vs. Bismark in *Kulturkampf,* 1871-87 (though concessions began in 1878). *LG*
5. Khilafat (Caliphate) satyagraha (India), 1920-22. *LG*
6. Akali Sikhs' reform satyagraha (India), 1922. *LG*
7. South Vietnam Buddhist campaign vs. Ngo Diem regime, 1963. *LG*

E. Against Particular Injustices and Administrative Excesses:
1. Economic boycotts, political noncooperation and tax refusal in American colonies, 1763-76. *LG*
2. Quebec farmers' and villagers' noncooperation with the British *corvée* system, 1776-78. *LG*
3. Persian anti-tobacco tax boycott, 1891. *LG*
4. German Social Democrats' struggle vs. Bismark, 1879-90. *LG*
5. Belgian general strikes for broader suffrage, 1893, 1902, and 1913. *LG*

6. Swedish three-day general strike for extension of suffrage, 1902. *LG*
7. English tax-refusal vs. tax aid for private schools, 1902-14. *LG*
8. Chinese anti-Japanese boycotts in 1906, 1908, 1915 and 1919. *LG*
9. "Free speech" campaign by Industrial Workers of the World in Sioux City, Iowa, 1914-15. *LG*
10. Kheda (India) peasants' resistance, 1918. *LG*
11. Peasants' passive resistance in USSR, post-1918. *LG*
12. Rowlatt Act satyagraha (India), 1919. *LG*
13. Bardoli (India) peasants' revenue refusal, 1928. *LG*
14. Pardi (India) satyagraha, 1950. *LG*
15. Manbhum, Bihar (India) resistance movement, 1950. *LG*
16. Nonviolent seizure of Heligoland from the Royal Air Force, 1951. *SM*
17. South Indian Telugu agitation for new state of Andra, pre-1953. *LG*
18. Political prisoners' strike at Vorkuta, USSR, 1953. *LG*
19. Finnish general strike, 1956. *LG*
20. African bus boycotts in Johannesburg, Pretoria, Port Elizabeth, and Bloemfontein, 1957. *LG*
21. Kerala (India) nonviolent resistance vs. elected Communist government's education policy, etc., 1959. *LG*
22. Argentine general strike, 1959. *LG*
23. Belgian general strike, 1960-61. *LG*

F. Against War and War Preparations:
1. New Zealand anti-conscription struggles, 1912-14 and 1930. *LG*
2. Argentine general strike vs. possible entry into World War I, 1917. *LG*
3. French, English, and Irish dock workers' strike against military intervention in Russia, 1920. *LG*
4. League of Nations' economic sanctions vs. Italy during war on Abyssinia, 1935-36. *LG*

5. Japanese resistance to constructing a U.S. air base at Sunakawa, 1956. *LG*
6. Various cases of civil disobedience and other nonviolent action in Britain in support of nuclear disarmament by the Direct Action Committee Against Nuclear War and the Committee of 100, 1958-63. *SM* and *LG*
7. Attempted "invasion" to prevent atomic test at Reggane, French North African atomic testing site, 1959-60. *SM*
8. Various cases of civil disobedience and other nonviolent action in the U.S. largely organized by the Committee for Nonviolent Action, 1959-66, including voyages of the *Golden Rule* and *Phoenix,* 1958, and of *Everyman I* and *Everyman II,* 1962, in efforts to stop U.S. nuclear tests in Pacific, and of *Everyman III* in protest against Soviet nuclear tests, 1962. *SM* and *LG*
9. Demonstration, threat of general strike, and various acts of nonviolent intervention between opposing troops to forestall civil war in newly-independent Algeria, August-September, 1962. *LG*

G. Against Long-established Undemocratic Rule:
1. Roman plebians vs. patricians, 494 B.C. *LG*
2. Major aspects of Netherlands' resistance vs. Spanish rule, especially 1565-76. *MX*
3. Hungarian passive resistance vs. Austria, 1850-67. *LG*
4. Finnish resistance to Russian rule, 1898-1905. *LG*
5. Major aspects of the 1905 revolution in Imperial Russia, including general strikes, parallel government, and various types of noncooperation. *MX*
6. Korean national protest vs. Japanese rule, 1919-22. *LG*
7. Egyptian passive resistance vs. British rule, 1919-22. *LG*

8. Western Samoan resistance vs. New Zealand rule, 1919-36. *LG*
9. Indian independence struggle, especially campaigns of 1930-31, 1932-34, 1940-41 and 1942. *LG*
10. Economic shut-down and political noncooperation in El Salvador vs. Martinez dictatorship, 1944. *LG*
11. Economic shut-down and political noncooperation in Guatemala vs. Ubico regime, 1944. *LG*
12. South African defiance campaign, 1952. *LG*
13. East German uprising, June, 1953. *LG (MX?)*
14. Nonviolent "invasion" of Goa, 1955. *LG*
15. General strike and economic shut-down vs. Haitian strong-man General Magliore, 1956. *LG*
16. Major aspects of the Hungarian revolution, 1956-57. *MX*
17. Barcelona and Madrid bus boycotts, 1957. *LG*
18. Nonviolent resistance to British rule in Nyasaland, *1957. LG*
19. South African Pan-Africanists' defiance of pass laws, 1960. *LG*
20. International boycotts and embargoes on South African products, from 1960. *LG*

H. Against New Attempts to Impose Undemocratic Rule: (Many of these actions were in support of the legitimate regime.)
1. Kanara (India) noncooperation, 1799-1800. *LG*
2. German general strike and political noncooperation vs. the Kapp *Putsch,* 1920. *LG*
3. Ruhr passive resistance vs. French and Belgian occupation, 1923. *LG*
4. Major aspects of the Dutch resistance, 1940-45, including several important strikes. *MX*
5. Major aspects of the Danish resistance, 1940-45, including the Copenhagen general strike, 1944. *MX*
6. Major aspects of the Norwegian resistance, 1940-45. *MX*

7. General strike in Haiti vs. temporary President Pierre-Louis, 1957. *LG*
8. British and U.N. economic sanctions vs. Rhodesia from 1965. *LG*
9. Popular resistance and demonstrations, and political noncooperation by Czechs and Slovaks following the Warsaw Pact invasion in August, 1968.

Forty-nine of these cases occurred in the "West" (including Russia); twenty-three in the "East" (including Samoa); nine in Africa; one in Australasia, and three are coordinated international actions. Something less than 40 per cent took place in "democracies" (roughly defined), and slightly more than 60 per cent under "dictatorships" (including foreign occupations and seven cases under totalitarian systems). In some of these cases the nonviolent actionists partly or fully succeeded in achieving the desired objectives; and in other cases — for example, many of the anti-war demonstrations — they failed. In not more than eight of these 85 cases have the leadership and participants been pacifist.

These rough classifications and comparisons are the closest that one comes in this study to comparative statistical analyses of the use and nature of the technique. This is largely because academic neglect of the subject has resulted in insufficient data for even preliminary statistical analysis.

Even making allowances for an incomplete and unrepresentative list, the above figures are sufficient to challenge seriously the conceptions that nonviolent action is mainly an "Eastern" phenomenon, that only "democratic" conditions would "allow" such action, that it is suitable only for convinced pacifists and that it ignores the existence of conflicts and power.

Various other common assumptions about nonviolent action are either destroyed or cast into severe doubt even by this list. Nonviolent action is, for example, not simply a weapon used by minority groups, but has also been used widely by majorities. This technique has been used to defend governments as well as to resist and oppose them. While most of the cases involve conflicts within the society or nation, a number of them occur in international conflicts, including national liberation and defense against foreign invasion. Sometimes nonviolent action has been used to achieve limited changes and reforms, while on other occasions the intent has been to replace the old regime with a new order. No one culture or part of the world seems to have either a particular propensity for, or against, the use of nonviolent action; this would be much clearer if the list were broadened by additional research to make it more representative.

A Course Program in Civilian Defense

by William B. Watson

Will Americans, who already have a vast experience in nonviolent action, recognize the enormous potential of nonviolent methods and consciously apply them in place of violence in the struggles that lie ahead? This, in my opinion, is the most urgent question now facing this country. It is by no means an easy question to answer. There are many voices who are prepared to denounce nonviolent alternatives as a cop-out, as ineffectual, as unrealistic in violence-prone America. There are others who are unwilling to try it because it seems too difficult, too demanding for them to carry off. But for most Americans, regardless of how often they may have engaged in nonviolent action, it remains an unknown subject. It is not that they are opposed to nonviolent alternatives. It is just that they know virtually nothing about them.

The program of courses in nonviolent action and civilian defense described in the following paragraphs attempts to meet this need for information. Somehow, and very quickly, people all over this country must be given a chance to see for themselves what nonviolent action can offer. The quickest and most effective way of doing this is to begin a series of courses in the universities and colleges of this country on various aspects of nonviolent action, from the methods of the technique to the implications of defense without armaments. There is already a sizable literature on the field — as shown in Chapter 7 — and more is appearing each day. Though the number of serious students of this technique in this country is small, there are thousands of people whose direct experience with nonviolent action has prepared them to begin exploring the subject with others. What is needed is some kind of program that will bring these people together so that the experience they have gained will not be lost. The program outlined below, or something like it, can be developed in a very short time on hundreds of campuses in this country.

Civilian defense, as this book makes clear, is a form of organized resistance based on the technique of nonviolent action. Its ultimate goal is to provide every person with the capacity to defend himself and his own interests as well as those of his group or society without at the same time taking the lives and destroying the property of his opponent. Its principal "weapon" is the collective action of its participants. Unlike military defense, it does not delegate the responsibility for defense to others, but relies on the capacity of each member of the group or society to contribute to the common objective of resistance. It assumes that the organization of defense will remain in the hands of those being defended.

The purpose of a program in civilian defense is therefore to prepare people to take action consistent with the principles and methods of nonviolent action. In order to carry out this purpose it must be able to offer an effective and realistic alternative to other forms of defense that rely upon violence and military force. It must be able to

Personal defense of one's own freedom taking the responsibility on yourself.

126

demonstrate the creative potential of the nonviolent technique in all kinds of conflict situations by drawing upon the considerable experience of nonviolent action in this country and elsewhere. It should be able to show that this technique is consistent with what we now understand to be the basic characteristics of individual and group behavior. A program such as this should also provide insights into the moral and political implications of nonviolent action and should explore, so far as possible, the social and political means needed to achieve the transition from military defense to civilian defense. Finally, a program in civilian defense must train participants in the specific means of nonviolent confrontation.

1. Methods and Dynamics of Nonviolent Action:

This basic course examines in detail the different methods of nonviolent action — the classes of symbolic protest, noncooperation and direct intevention — the strategies and tactics of their employment, and how nonviolent action works. The course has three objectives: 1) to show the great variety of methods available to nonviolent actionists and the degree of difficulty and commitment required by each one; 2) to acquaint participants with the vast historical experience of nonviolent action; and 3) to gain understanding of how this technique produces change, uses the opponent's repression to its own advantage and alters power relationships. Questions which this course should try to raise are going to be numerous, especially if it is taught as a beginning course, but a few general questions will come up throughout the course. How feasible is nonviolent action? How does it work against repression? What leverages does it apply? What are its probable effects on both participants and opponents? What problems and risks are involved in its application to specific conflict situations? These and other questions are best raised in the context of actual case histories. *127*

2. Civilian Defense:

This course engages the whole range of questions that will immediately arise when one is asked to think of how large numbers of people or entire countries can use social, economic, and political power as an alternative to military power in defending themselves against external aggression, internal violence, or political repression. The course is intended not only to look at the various alternatives to military defense, but to compare those alternatives with the consequences of military defense in the twentieth century. Of course the first question is going to be whether civilian defense offers a realistic alternative to military defense, but it might just as well be put the other way around. Is military defense a realistic alternative for most of the world's population? How successful has the military actually been in defending civilian populations? What is it that is being defended? Such questions make easier evaluation of civilian defense as a viable alternative. Case histories of unprepared national resistance (as Czechoslovakia) can be used, but a good deal of the effectiveness of this course will depend on the ability of participants to make realistic projections for completely new situations. Proceeding from the existing literature, attention will be given to such problems as these: the "transarmament" period, training and preparations of the whole population, distinctive defense problems against various types of attack, alternative strategies and tactics, questions of general and organized resistance, resistance roles of special groups, and strategies for destroying the usurpation. (A basic course).

3. The History of Resistance:

The history of resistance could well be the history of any society at certain moments in its past, but it should also include the history of minority groups and oppressed peoples, much of whose history has either been ignored or suppressed by the dominant culture. The subject includes both violent and nonviolent forms of resistance and the failures as well as the successes. Some of the questions that deserve particular attention are the following: How was the resistance organized and conducted? What were the effects of violent and nonviolent tactics on the outcome? What were the causes of success or failure of specific resistance movements? Again, case histories from primarily the twentieth century dealing with specific acts of resistance as well as with large-scale resistance movements should provide the basic materials for this course.

4. The Moral and Political Bases of Nonviolence:

Nonviolence is viewed by most people as a moral principle demanding certain religious or ethical assumptions of the practitioner, but the fact is that nonviolent action has been used by many more people as a political technique without subscribing to any particular religious or ethical code. The differences between these views and their relationships to each other is the subject matter of this course. The main objective of this course is to examine the different levels of understanding and commitment required for nonviolent action. Questions such as: Is nonviolence an all-or-nothing kind of proposition? Can nonviolent action be used for political objectives in a society that has little understanding of nonviolence? Can people with different assumptions about nonviolence participate together in nonviolent action? Much of the literature deals with these and other related questions, but the experience of Gandhi is particularly revealing.

5. Aggression, Violence, and Self-defense:

The question of whether nonviolent social behavior is consistent with what we now understand about the basic characteristics of individuals and groups is taken up by this course. The evidence of anthropology, psychology, and sociology is examined for the insights these disciplines may provide on the question of man's capacity for self-defense. *129*

Is it rooted in some form of institutional behavior? Is it affected by different social and political institutions? What assumptions, if any, must one make about human behavior in constructing a viable form of defense?

6. The Politics of Defense:

The premise of this course is that societies with different forms of defense will require different kinds of political and social institutions. This premise is tested by looking at different defense systems and the societies that created them, as well as by projecting the kinds of social and political institutions that would be required for the development and maintaining of civilian defense. The underlying question is how power is distributed and controlled by each of these societies, but the course should raise other questions related to this one, such as: What are the social costs and benefits of each form of defense? What are the kinds of controls which are maintained over each system?

7. Post-military Society:

How to make the transition from military defense to civilian defense is the question raised by this course. The economic consequences of moving from a military-dominated budget to a civilian-oriented budget, the social resources needed to effect the conversion of military activities into peaceful activities, the amount of control and planning that might be involved in making such a change and the various ways it might be carried out are some of the subjects included in this course. Emphasis will be given to the various ways this change might be carried out. What are the alternative phased programs for training the people and for other preparations? How long a period would be required? How would the problems of building up civilian defense capacity and phasing out military capacity be solved? The objective of the course is to provide an awareness of the vast implications of converting from military to civilian defense as well as some insights into how it might actually be carried out.

8. Nonviolent Confrontation:

Training in specific methods of nonviolent action is intended to provide participants in the program with concrete notions of what may be required of them in particular kinds of confrontation — with the police, with a hostile group, with disruptive individuals within a group of demonstrators, etc. Questions on how to organize and train people for nonviolent action under various conditions, how to maintain communication and discipline, how to prepare for mass demonstrations, and other practical matters related to the carrying out of nonviolent actions will be taken up by the course.

7

Selected
Further Readings

POLITICAL POWER: ITS NATURE AND CONTROL

Sharp, *The Politics of Nonviolent Action,* Chapter I.

STUDIES OF THE TECHNIQUE OF
NONVIOLENT ACTION

1. Basic Study on Nonviolent Action

Gene Sharp, *The Politics of Nonviolent Action: An
Encyclopedia of Thought and Action* (900 or more
pages). Introduction by Prof. Thomas C. Schelling.
Prepared under the auspices of Harvard University's
Center for International Affairs. Published by Pilgrim
Press, Philadelphia, 1971, hardcover and paperback.
For price information, contact Pilgrim Press, 1505
Race Street, Philadelphia, Pa. 19102.   *133*

2. Terminology and Concepts

Gene Sharp, *An Abecedary of Nonviolent Action and Civilian Defense,* app. 124 pp., Cambridge, Mass. Schenkman Publishing Co., November, 1970 (hardcover $3.95, paperback $1.95). For quantity prices, contact Schenkman, 1 Story Street, Cambridge, Mass. 02138.

3. Recommended Bibliographies

April Carter, David Hoggett, and Adams Roberts (eds), *Nonviolent Action: A Selected Bibliography* (revised and enlarged edition), 84 pp., London, Housmans, 1970, and Haverford, Pa., Center for Nonviolent Conflict Resolution, Haverford College ($1.50).

Robert Pickus and Robert Woito, *To End War: An Introduction to the Ideas, Organizations, and Current Books* (new edition), New York, Harper & Row, September, 1970. (Items in print in this bibliography, including unusual ones, are available from World Without War Council, 1730 Grove Street, Berkeley, Cal. 94709.)

4. Short Introduction to Nonviolent Action

Gene Sharp, *A Handbook of Nonviolent Action* (tentative title of an abridgement of *The Politics of Nonviolent Action*), app. 200 pp., Philadelphia, Pilgrim Press, 1971.

5. General Studies of Nonviolence and Nonviolent Action

Clarence Marsh Case, *Non-Violent Coercion: A Study in Methods of Social Pressure,* 422 pp., New York, Century Co., 1923, and London, Allen & Unwin, 1923.

April Carter, *Direct Action,* 34 pp. (pamphlet). London, Peace News, 1962 and later.

Anthony de Crespigny, "The Nature and Methods of Nonviolent Coercion," in *Political Studies,* (London) Vol. XII, No. 2, June, 1964, pp. 256-265.

A. Paul Hare and Herbert H. Blumberg (eds.), *Nonviolent Direct Action: American Cases: Social-Psychological Analysis,* 575 pp., Washington, D.C., Corpus Books (hardcover $10.00).

Barthelemy de Ligt, *The Conquest of Violence: An Essay on War and Revolution,* New York, E. P. Dutton, 1938, and London, Routledge, 1937.

Staughton Lynd (ed), *Nonviolence in America: A Documentary History,* 535 pp., Indianapolis *et al.,* Bobb-Merrill Co., 1965 (hardcover $7.50, paperback $3.45).

William Robert Miller, *Nonviolence: A Christian Interpretation,* New York, Association Press, 1964, and London, Allen & Unwin, 1964. (Case material in last part of this book.) Also published in paperback, New York, Schocken Books, Inc., 1966 ($2.45).

Mulford Q. Sibley (ed), *The Quiet Battle: Writings on the Theory and Practice of Non-Violent Resistance,* 390 pp., Boston, Beacon Press, 1969 (paperback $2.95).

Some of these are oriented toward principled nonviolence, or involve mixtures of that and the technique approach. Most contain some case material and bibliography or footnote reference.

6. History of Nonviolent Action

Sharp, *The Politics of Nonviolent Action,* Chapter 2.
Case, *Non-Violent Coercion (op. cit.).*
de Ligt, *The Conquest of Violence (op.cit.).*
Also see books on specific methods (strikes, etc.) and specific cases. There is no good history of this technique.

7. Methods of Nonviolent Action

Basic:
Sharp, *The Politics of Nonviolent Action,* Part II (detailed classification, definitions, and historical examples).

Civil disobedience:
Hugh Adam Bedau (ed), *Civil Disobedience: Theory and*   *135*

Practice, 282 pp., New York, Pegasus, 1969 (hardcover $7.50, paperback $1.95).

Abe Fortas, *Concerning Dissent and Civil Disobedience,* 68 pp., New York, New American Library, 1968 (hardcover $4.00, paperback $ .60).

Robert A. Goldwin (ed), *On Civil Disobedience: American Essays, Old and New,* 145 pp., Chicago, Rand McNally & Co., 1969 (paperback $1.95).

Sharp, "Civil Disobedience in a Democracy," Peace News reprint, 17 pp., London, Housmans, 1968.

Henry David Thoreau, *On the Duty of Civil Disobedience,* 21 pp., London, Peace News, 1963. (Introduction by Gene Sharp.)

Howard Zinn, *Disobedience and Democracy,* 124 pp., New York, Random House, 1968 (hardcover $3.95, Vintage Books paperback $1.45). (This is a reply to Fortas. Zinn incorrectly asserts civil disobedience may be violent.)

Economic Boycotts:

John A. Fitch, "Strikes and Lockouts," *Encyclopedia of the Social Sciences,* Vol. IV, New York, Macmillan, 1931.

Harry Laidler, "Boycott," *Encyclopedia of the Social Sciences,* Vol. II, pp. 662-666.

————, *Boycotts and the Labor Struggle,* New York, Russell & Russell, 1968 (1913), (hardcover $12.50).

Leo Wolman, *The Boycott in American Trade Unions,* 147 pp., John Hopkins University Studies in Historical & Political Science, Series XXXIV No. 1, 1916. (Important historical background.)

See also sources cited in these; also in Sharp, The Politics of Nonviolent Action, *and in citations under individual methods and international economic sanctions.*

International economic sanctions:

136 G. W. Baer, *The Coming of the Italian-Ethiopian War,*

Cambridge, Mass., Harvard University Press, 1967 (hardcover $9.50). (See especially chapter 12.)

Evans Clark (ed), *Boycotts and Peace: A Report by the Committee on Economic Sanctions,* 381 pp., New York and London, Harper & Bros., 1932.

Johan Galtung, "On the Effects of International Economic Sanctions with Examples from the Case of Rhodesia," in *World Politics,* Vol. XIX, No. 3 (April, 1967), pp. 378-416.

Frederick Hoffman, "The Functions of Economic Sanctions: A Comparative Analysis," in *Journal of Peace Research,* Oslo, No. 2, 1967, pp. 140-160.

Amelia C. Leiss (ed), *Apartheid and United Nations Collective Measures,* New York, Carnegie Endowment for International Peace, 1965.

The Royal Institute of International Affairs, *International Sanctions,* London *et al.,* Oxford University Press, 1938.

Ronald Segal (ed), *Sanctions Against South Africa,* Harmondsworth, Middlesex, Baltimore, *et al.,* Penguin Books, 1964.

Rita Faulk Taubenfeld and Howard J. Taubenfeld, "The 'Economic Weapon': The League and the United Nations," in *Proceedings of the American Society of International Law,* 1964, pp. 183-205.

Peter Wallensteen, "Characteristics of Economic Sanctions," in *Journal of Peace Research,* Oslo, No. 3, 1968, pp. 248-267.

F. P. Walters, *A History of the League of Nations,* London, Oxford University Press, 1960 (hardcover $11.50).

Strikes:

Wilfred H. Crook, *Communism and the General Strike,* Hamden, Conn., The Shoestring Press, 1960. (Both this and the following contain important historical material.)

————, *The General Strike: A Study of Labor's Tragic Weapon in Theory and Practice,* Chapel Hill, University

137

of North Carolina Press, 1931.

E. T. Hiller, *The Strike,* New York, Arno, 1969, (1928) (hardcover $11.00). (A classic.)

K. G. J. C. Knowles, *Strikes — A Study in Industrial Conflict with Special Reference to British Experience Between 1911 and 1945,* New York, Philosophical Library, 1952, and Oxford, Basil Blackwell, 1954.

A. P. Lindsey, *The Pullman Strike,* Chicago, University of Chicago Press, 1942 (paperback $2.95).

J. P. Rayback, *The History of American Labor,* New York, The Free Press, 1946 (paperback $3.50).

Julian Symons, *The General Strike: A Historical Portrait,* Chester Springs, Pa., Dufour, 1957, and London, The Cresset Press, 1957. (The British general strike of 1926.)

Sidney and Beatrice Webb, *The History of Trade Unionism,* New York, Kelley, 1965 (1894) (hardcover $12.50).

Samuel Yellon, *American Labor Struggles,* New York, Russell Press, 1956, and New York, Arno, 1964 (hardcover $14).

David Ziskind, *One Thousand Strikes of Government Employees,* New York, Columbia University Press, 1940.

Also check sources cited in various of these books, and histories of particular unions, unionism in particular countries, and particular cases, such as Russia 1905 and 1917, German resistance to the Kapp Putsch, *the* Ruhrkampf, *etc.*

8. The Dynamics of Nonviolent Action

Basic:

Gene Sharp, *The Politics of Nonviolent Action, Part III.* (The working of "political *jiu-jitsu*," and the factors influencing the outcome by mechanisms of conversion, accommodation, and nonviolent coercion.)

Shorter studies:

Richard Gregg, *The Power of Non-violence,* 187 pp., New York, Schoken paperback, 1966, and London, James Clarke, 1960 (hardcover $5, paperback $1.95). (A revision of his 1934 book, emphasizing conversion of the opponent.)

Herbert Kelman, *A Time to Speak: On Human Values and Social Research,* San Francisco, Jossey-Bass, 1968. (See especially Chapter 9: "The Relevance of Nonviolent Action.")

George R. Lakey, "The Sociological Mechanisms of Nonviolent Action," 104 pp., in *Peace Research Reviews,* Vol. II, No. 6 (December, 1968), Oakville, Ontario, Canadian Peace Research Institute. (His MA thesis, sketching the three basic mechanisms of change; an advance on Gregg.)

Irving L. Janis and Daniel Katz, "The Reduction of Inter-group Hostility: Research Problems and Hypotheses," in *Journal of Conflict Resolution,* Vol. III, No. 1 (March, 1959), pp. 85-100, Ann Arbor, Michigan. (Social psychologists look at Gandhi's norms of action.)

Harvey Seifert, *Conquest by Suffering: The Process and Prospects of Nonviolent Resistance,* 207 pp., Philadelphia, Westminster Press, 1965. (Emphasizes love and conversion.)

Examine also specific cases of nonviolent struggle, and particular methods, such as strikes, for important supplementary material.

9. Handbooks on organizing nonviolent action

Martin Oppenheimer and George Lakey, *A Manual for Direct Action: Strategy and Tactics for Civil Rights and All Other Nonviolent Protest Movements,* 139 pp., Chicago, Quadrangle Books, 1965.

Charles C. Walker, "Organizing for Civil Disobedience" (mimeo), 13 pp., Washington, New Mobilization, 1970;   *139* available from the author, Box 125, Haverford College, Haverford, Penna. 19041.

Charles C. Walker, *Organizing for Nonviolent Direct Action*, 31 pp., Cheyney, Penna., the author, 1961.

These are now either rather dated, or otherwise limited in focus. The basic action manual remains yet to be written.

10. Nonviolent Revolution

David Dellinger, *Revolutionary Nonviolence*, 390 pp., New York and Indianapolis, Bobbs-Merrill, 1970 (hardcover $7.50).

Barbara Deming and Regis Debray, "Revolution: Violent and Nonviolent," 28 pp., *Liberation Reprint*, 1964 ($ .35).

Mulford Q. Sibley, "Revolution and Violence," 8 pp., *Peace News* reprint ($ .10).

Both of the above are available from the World Without War Council. See also rare sources cited in footnotes to the section on nonviolent revolution in G. Sharp, "Types of Principled Nonviolence," listed on page 158.

11. Civilian Defense

Introductory:

American Friends Service Committee, *In Place of War: An Inquiry into Unarmed National Defense*, 115 pp., New York, Grossman, 1967 (hardcover $3.95, paperback $1.45). (A rather optimistic introduction.)

T. K. Mahadevan, Adams Roberts, and Gene Sharp (eds), *Civilian Defence: An Introduction*, 265 pp., Bombay, Bharatiya Vidya Bhavan and New Delhi, Gandhi Peace Foundation, 1967 (U.S. price $4.95).

Gene Sharp, "The Political Equivalent of War" — Civilian Defense, 67 pp., *International Conciliation*, No. 555 (November, 1965, whole issue), New York, Carnegie Endowment for International Peace.

Basic:

Adams Roberts (ed), *Civilian Resistance as a National*

Defense: Nonviolent Action Against Aggression, 320 pp., Harrisburg, Pa., Stackpole Books, 1968 (hardcover $7.95). Original title: *The Strategy of Civilian Defense,* London, Faber and Faber, 1967. Paper edition titled: *Civilian Resistance as a National Defense,* 367 pp., A Pelican Book ($1.65), Harmondsworth, Middlesex, England, and Baltimore, Md., Penguin Books, 1969.
See larger listing, predominantly of earlier publications, in Nonviolent Action: A Selected Bibliography.

"HUMAN NATURE," SOCIAL CONFLICT, AND THE ELIMINATION OF WAR

12. Psychological Aspects

Leonard Berkowitz (ed), *Roots of Aggression: A Re-examination of the Frustration-Aggression Hypothesis,* 136 pp., New York, Atherton Press, 1969 (hardcover $6.95, paperback $2.95).

Jerome D. Frank, *Sanity and Survival: Psychological Aspects of War and Peace,* New York, Random House, 1968 (hardcover $5.95, paperback $1.95).

Jerome D. Frank, "Breaking the Thought Barrier: Psychological Challenges of the Nuclear Age," in Thomas Merton (ed), *Breakthrough to Peace: Twelve Views on the Threat of Thermonuclear Extermination,* pp. 206-249, Norfolk, Conn., and New York, New Directions, 1962.

Group for the Advancement of Psychiatry, Report #57, *Psychiatric Aspects of the Prevention of Nuclear War,* 94 pp., 1964 ($1.50).

Konrad Lorenz, *On Aggression,* 306 pp., New York, Harcourt, Brace & World, 1963 (hardcover $5.95), and Bantam Paperback ($1.45).

M. F. Ashley Montagu (ed), *Man and Aggression,* 178 pp., New York, Oxford University Press, 1968 (hardcover $5.00, paperback $1.95). (A necessary supplement to Lorenz.)

13. Sociology of Conflict

Joan V. Bondurant (ed), *Conflict: Violence and Nonviolence,* 200 pp., New York, Atherton Press, 1970 (hardcover $6.95, paperback $2.45).

Leon Bramson and George W. Goethals, *War: Studies from Psychology, Sociology, Anthropology,* 406 pp., New York and London, Basic Books, 1964 (hardcover $10, paperback $4.95). (See especially Bronislaw Malinowski's chapter, "An Anthropological Analysis of War.")

Lewis Coser, *The Functionsof Social Conflict,* New York, Free Press of Glencoe, 1956 (text edition $6.50, paperback $1.95).

Morton Fried, Marvin Harris, and Robert Murphy, *War: The Anthropology of Armed Conflict and Aggression,* 262 pp., Garden City, N.Y., Natural History Press, 1968 (paperback $3.50).

Elton B. McNeil (ed), *The Nature of Human Conflict,* Englewood Cliffs, N.J., Prentice-Hall, Inc., 1965 (hardcover $7.95).

T. H. Pear, R. Aron, and R. C. Angell (eds), *The Nature of Conflict,* Paris, UNESCO, 1957.

CASES OF NONVIOLENT ACTION

14. American Colonial Nonviolent Resistance

Lawrence Henry Gipson, *The British Empire Before the American Revolution* (Vol. X, *The Triumphant Empire: Thunder Clouds Gather in the West, 1763-1766;* Vol. XI, *The Triumphant Empire: The Rumbling of the Coming Storm, 1766-1770;* Vol. XII, *The Triumphant Empire: Britain Sails into the Storm, 1770-1776*), New York, Alfred A. Knopf, 1961-65 ($10 per volume).

Merrill Jensen, *The Founding of a Nation: A History of the American Revolution, 1763-1776,* 735 pp., New York, Oxford University Press, 1968 ($13.50).

Edmund S. and Helen M. Morgan, *The Stamp Act Crisis,* Chapel Hill, N.C., The University of North Carolina Press, 1953 (hardcover $7.50); new revised edition: *The Stamp Act Crisis: Prologue to Revolution,* New York, Collier Books, 1963 (paperback $1.50).

Arthur M. Schlesinger, *The Colonial Merchants and the American Revolution, 1763-1776,* New York, Frederick Ungar, 1966 (hardcover $10.50), and New York, Atheneum, 1968 (paperback $4.95).

15. Nonviolent Action Against Slavery

Carleton Mabee, *Black Freedom: The Nonviolent Abolitionists from 1830 Through the Civil War,* 435 pp., New York, Macmillan; Toronto, The Macmillan Co.; and London, Collier-Macmillan Ltd., 1970 (hardcover $8.95).

16. Hungary, 1849-1867

Arthur Griffith, *The Resurrection of Hungary: A Parallel for Ireland,* 170 pp., Dublin, Whelan & Son, 1918.

Brabourne, C. M. Knatchbull-Hugessen, 4th Baron, *The Political Evolution of the Hungarian Nation,* Vol. II (chapters XVI-XIX), London, National Review Office, 1908.

A. J. P. Taylor, *The Hapsburg Monarchy, 1809-1918,* New York, Harper & Row, 1941 (hardcover $5 and Torch paperback $1.95). Also published in paperback (304 pp.) by Penguin Books, Harmondsworth, Middlesex, and Baltimore, Md., 1964.

Leo Valiani, *The End of Austria Hungary,* London, Secker and Warburg, 1970.

17. Finland, 1898-1905

J. Hampden Jackson, *Finland,* New York, Macmillan, and London, Allen & Unwin, 1938. (See chapters 4 and 5 and bibliography.)

Eino Jutikkala, *A History of Finland,* New York, Frederick A. Praeger, 1962, and London, Thames and Hudson, 1962 (hardcover $7.75). (See chapters 8 and 9.)

Anatole G. Mazour, *Finland Between East and West,* Princeton, N.J., D. Van Nostrand Co., 1956. (See pages 11-27 and bibliography.)

18. Russia, 1905-1906

Richard Charques, *The Twilight of Imperial Russia,* London, Oxford University Press, 1965 (paperback $2.25). (See section on 1905.)

Sidney Harcave, *First Blood: The Russian Revolution of 1905,* New York, Macmillan 1968, and London, Collier-Macmillan, 1964 (hardcover $5.75). Paperback by Collier-Macmillan, New York, retitled: *Russian Revolution of Nineteen Hundred-Five* ($2.95).

V. I. Lenin, "Lecture on the 1905 Revolution," in *Lenin, Selected Works in Three Volumes,* Vol. I, pp. 788-802, New York, International Publishers, 1967 (three-volume paperback set $9.95).

Henry W. Nevinson, *The Dawn in Russia, or Scenes in the Russian Revolution,* London and New York, Harper & Bros. 1906.

Leonard Schapiro, *The Communist Party of the Soviet Union,* New York, Random House, and London, Eyre and Spottiswoode, 1960, (hardcover $7.50, paperback $2.65). (See pages 63-70 and 85.)

Solomon M. Schwartz, *The Russian Revolution of 1905: The Workers' Movement and the Formation of Bolshevism and Menshevism,* Chicago and London, University of Chicago Press, 1967. (See pages 129-195.)

Hugh Seton-Watson, *The Decline of Imperial Russia,* New York, Praeger, and London, Methuen, 1952 (hardcover $8.50, paperback $2.95). (See pages 219-260.)

Bertram D. Wolfe, *Three Who Made a Revolution* (fourth ed.), New York, Dial Press, 1964 (hardcover $7.50),

and London, Thames and Hudson, 1956 (pp. 278-336).
Also published as Dell paperback, New York ($2.95).

19. Russia, February — March 1917

George Katkov, *Russia 1917: The February Revolution,*
489 pp., New York, Harper & Row, 1967 ($8.50).

Leon Trotsky, *History of the Russian Revolution,* 1295
pp., Ann Arbor, University of Michigan Press, 1957
($14.50) and London, Gollancz, 1965. (See chapters
7-9 of Volume I.)

20. Germany, 1920

Wilfred Harris Crook, *The General Strike (op. cit.)* pp.
496-527.

D. J. Goodspeed, *The Conspirators: A Study in the Coup
d'Etat,* New York, Viking Press, and Toronto,
Macmillan Co. of Canada, 1962. (See especially pp.
108-143 and 211-213.) Paperback Canadian edition
available.

S. William Halperin, *Germany Tried Democracy: A
Political History of the Reich from 1918 to 1933,*
Hamden, Conn., and London, Archon Books, 1965,
(1946). (See pp. 168-188.) Paperback edition by
Norton, New York ($2.75).

Erich Eyck, *A History of the Weimar Republic,* Vol. I,
Cambridge, Mass., Harvard University Press, 1962
(hardcover $10). (See pp. 129-160.) Also New York,
Atheneum (paperback $3.25).

Robert G. L. Waite, *Vanguard of Nazism: The Free Corps
Movement in Postwar Germany, 1918-1923,*
Cambridge, Mass., Harvard University Press, 1952. Also
New York, Norton, 1969 (paperback $1.95). (See
chapter VI.)

See also the bibliographies in these studies.

20. The Ruhr, 1923

Erich Eych, *A History of the Weimer Republic,* Vol. I *(op.
cit.),* pp. 232-306 passim.

G. E. R. Gedye, *The Revolver Republic: France's Bid for the Rhine*, 255 pp., London, Arrowsmith, 1930.

Halperin, *Germany Tried Democracy (op. cit.)*, pp. 246-260 and 288-289.

Wolfgang Sternstein, "The *Ruhrkampf* of 1923," chapter 5 in Roberts (ed), *Civilian Resistance as a National Defense* (see page 140). See also the German bibliography cited by Sternstein, and further items in *Nonviolent Action: A Selected Bibliography.*

Arnold J. Toynbee, *Survey of International Affairs, 1924*, London, Oxford University Press, 1928, pp. 268-300.

Ferdinand Tuohy, *Occupied 1918-1930: A Postscript to the Western Front*, London, Thornton Butterworth, 1931. (See chapter XVI.)

21. Gandhi

Biographies:

Geoffrey Ashe, *Gandhi: A Study in Revolution,* New York, Stein & Day, 1969 (494 pp.), and London, Heinemann, 1968 (404 pp.) (hardcover $8.95, paperback $3.95).

Louis Fischer, *Gandhi: His Life and Message for the World,* 192 pp., New York, Mentor, New American Library, 1954 ($ .75).

_____ , *The Life of Mahatma Gandhi,* 593 pp., New York, Harper & Bros., 1950, and London, Jonathan Cape, 1951 ($10).

B. R. Nanda, *Mahatma Gandhi* (abridged), 272 pp., Woodbury, N.Y., Barron, 1969 (hardcover $3.95, paperback $ .95).

_____ , *Mahatma Gandhi: A Biography,* 542 pp., Boston, Beacon Press, 1958, and London, Allen and Unwin, 1958.

Robert Payne, *The Life and Death of Mahatma Gandhi,* 703 pp., New York, Dutton, 1969, and London, the Bodley Head, 1969 ($12.95).

Analyses:

Joan V. Bondurant, *Conquest of Violence: The Gandhian Philosophy of Conflict,* 269 pp., (paperback edition, 261 pp.), Berkeley California, University of California Press, 1965 (hardcover $4.50, paperback $1.95).

Gopi Nath Dhawan, *The Political Philosophy of Mahatma Gandhi,* Ahmedabad, Navajivan, 1962.

Ranganath R. Diwaker, *Saga of Satyagraha,* New Delhi, Gandhi Peace Foundation, and Bombay, Baratiya Vidya Bhavan, 1969.

Erik Erikson, *Gandhi's Truth: On the Origins of Militant Nonviolence,* 474 pp., New York, W. W. Norton & Co., 1969, and London, Faber & Faber, 1970 (hardcover $10, text edition $2.95).

H. J. N. Horsburg, *Non-violence and Aggression: A Study of Gandhi's Moral Equivalent of War,* 207 pp., London, Oxford University Press, 1968.

G. Ramachandran and T. K. Mahadevan (eds), *Gandhi: His Relevance for Our Times* (rev. ed.), New Delhi, Gandhi Peace Foundation, 1967. U.S. paperback edition: Berkeley, World Without War Council, 1970 ($2.95).

Krishnalal Shridharani, *War Without Violence: A Study of Gandhi's Method and Its Accomplishment,* New York, Harcourt Brace & Co., 1939, and London, Gollancz, 1939. New Indian revised edition (1962) available from World Without War Council (380 pp., $1.50).

Struggles:

Mahadev Desai, *The Story of Bardoli: Being a History of the Bardoli Satyagraha of 1928 and Its Sequel,* 249 pp., Ahmedabad, Navajivan, 1957 (1929).

M. K. Gandhi, *Satyagraha in South Africa,* 348 pp., 1964. Available from the World Without War Council ($2.00).

S. Gopal, *The Viceroyalty of Lord Irwin, 1926-1931,* 152 pp., London, Oxford University Press, 1957.

Jawaharlal Nehru, *An Autobiography,* New York, Paragon Press, 1965 (paperback $2.50).

_____, *Toward Freedom,* New York, John Day Co., 1942. Paperback edition: Boston, Beacon Press ($2.45). (A shortened version of Nehru's Autobiography.)

Simone Panter-Brick, *Gandhi Against Machiavellism: Nonviolence in Politics,* 240 pp., Bombay, London, New York, *et al.,* Asia Publishing Co., 1966.

Bhagaraju Pattabhi Sitamarayya, *The History of the Indian National Congress, 1885-1935,* Vol. I, Madras, Working Committee of the Congress, 1935.

Gene Sharp, *Gandhi Wields the Weapon of Moral Power,* 316 pp., Ahmedabad, Navajivan, 1960. (Gopal's account of the 1930-31 struggle should be read with the account here. This also contains Champaran and the 1948 Delhi fast.)

Check also Erikson's Gandhi's Truth *on the Ahmedabad strike, biographies of Gandhi for sketches of various campaigns, and, for longer accounts as beginnings for historical studies: D. G. Tendulkar,* Mahatma: Life of Mohandas Karamchand Gandhi *(eight volumes), Delhi, Ministry of Information and Broadcasting, 1962.*

Writings:

Nirmal Kumar Bose (ed), *Selections from Gandhi,* 320 pp., Available from World Without War Council ($2.50).

M. K. Gandhi, *All Men Are Brothers,* 253 pp., compiled for UNESCO by Krishan Kriplani, 1968. Available from World Without War Council ($1.95).

_____, *Non-violent Resistance,* New York, Schoken Books, 1967 (hardcover $4.50, paperback $1.95). Indian edition: *Satyagraha,* Ahmedabad, Navajivan, 1951. (Collected articles and summaries of speeches on the use of the nonviolent technique.)

_____, *Non-violence in Peace and War,* two volumes, Ahmedabad, Navajivan, 1948 and 1949. (Important collected writings covering a long period.)

————, *Satyagraha in South Africa,* Ahmedabad, Navajivan, 1951.

Thomas Merton (ed), *Gandhi on Non-violence: Selected Texts from Gandhi's Non-violence in Peace and War,* New York, New Directions paperback, 1965 ($1.50).

Bibliography:

Jagdish Sharma, *Mahatma Gandhi: A Descriptive Bibliography,* 650 pp., Delhi, S. Chand, 1968.

23. Khan Abdul Ghaffar Khan
and the Muslim "Servants of God"

C. F. Andrews, *The Challenge of the North-West Frontier,* London, Allen & Unwin, 1937.

Joan V. Bondurant, *Conquest of Violence (op. cit.),* pp. 131-144.

Pyarelal (Nayar), *Thrown to the Wolves,* Calcutta, Eastlight Book House, 1966.

James W. Spain, *The Way of the Pathans,* London, Robert Hale, 1962.

D. G. Tendulkar, *Abdul Ghaffar Khan: Faith Is a Battle,* 550 pp., Bombay, Popular Prakashan, for the Gandhi Peace Foundation, 1967.

Mohammad Yunus, *Frontier Speaks,* Bombay, Hind Kitabs, 1947.

24. Nazi-Occupied Europe

General:

E. K. Bramstedt, *Dictatorship and Political Police: The Technique of Control by Fear,* 275 pp., London, Kegan Paul, Trench, Trubner & Co., 1945. (See especially chapter VI.)

European Resistance Movements, 1939-1945: First International Conference on the History of the Resistance Movements held . . . 1958, 410 pp., Oxford, Pergamon Press, 1960.

European Resistance Movements, 1939-1945 (Volume II): *Proceedings of the Second International Conference on the History of Resistance Movements held . . . 1961,* 663 pp., Oxford, Pergamon Press, 1964.

B. H. Liddell Hart, "Lessons from Resistance Movements — Guerrilla and Nonviolent," chapter 9 in Roberts (ed), *Civilian Resistance as a National Defense* (see page 140).

Curt Riess, *Underground Europe,* 325 pp., New York, Dial Press, 1942.

Arnold and Veronica M. Toynbee (eds), *Survey of International Affairs, 1939-1946: Hitler's Europe,* 730 pp., London *et al.,* Oxford University Press, 1954 ($12). (See especially parts IV-VI.)

Denmark:

Jeremy Bennett, *British Broadcasting and the Danish Resistance Movement, 1940-45,* 266 pp., Cambridge at the University Press, 1966.

————, "The Resistance Against the German Occupation of Denmark, 1940-45," chapter 7 in Roberts (ed), *Civilian Resistance as a National Defense* (see page 140).

Aage Bertelsen, *October '43,* 160 pp., London, Museum Press, 1955. (Resistance against deportation of Jews.)

Harold Flender, *Rescue in Denmark,* 281 pp., New York, Simon and Schuster, 1963, and London, W. H. Allen, 1963. Also available in paperback: New York, Macfadden ($ .75). (Also on anti-deportation resistance; reportedly contains some errors.)

David Lampe, *The Savage Canary: The Story of Resistance in Denmark,* 236 pp., London, Cassell, 1957.

Jewish:

Juri Suhl (ed), *They Fought Back: The Story of the Jewish Resistance in Nazi Europe,* 327 pp., New York, Crown, 1967 ($5.95), and London, Macgibbon and Kee, 1968.

Available in paperback: New York, Paperback Library ($ .75). (Covers both violent and nonviolent resistance. Note especially the bibliography.)

Netherlands:

Louis de Jong and J. W. F. Stoppelman, *The Lion Rampant: The Story of Holland's Resistance to the Nazis,* 336 pp., New York, Querido, 1943.

Nicolaas Wilhelmus Posthumus (ed), "The Netherlands During German Occupation," in *The Annals of the American Academy of Political and Social Science,* 231 pp., Vol. 245 (May, 1964), Philadelphia, Pa.

Warner Warmbrunn, *The Dutch Under German Occupation, 1940-1945,* Stanford, Cal., Stanford University Press, and London, Oxford University Press, 1963 ($7.50). (Contains a bibliography.)

See also publications of the Netherlands State Institute for War Documentation, mostly in Dutch, frequently with English summaries.

Norway:

Johannes Andernaes, Olav Riste, and Magne Skodvin, *Norway and the Second World War,* 168 pp., Oslo, Johan Grundt Tanum, 1966.

Magne Skodvin, "Norway in the Second World War," in Harald L. Tveteras (ed), *Humaniora Norvegica: The Year's Work in Norwegian Humanities,* 1950, 252 pp., Oslo, Akademisk Forlag, 1954. (With bibliography.)

————, "Norwegian Nonviolent Resistance During the German Occupation," chapter 6 in Roberts (ed), *Civilian Resistance as a National Defence (op. cit.)*

Gene Sharp, "Tyranny Could Not Quell Them: How Norway's Teachers Defeated Quisling . . ." 43-page pamphlet, London, Peace News, 1963 (1959).

On all of World War II resistance, see also titles listed in Nonviolent Action: A Selected Bibliography.

25. Guatemala, 1944

Mario Rosenthal, *Guatemala: The Story of an Emergent Latin-American Democracy,* New York, Twayne, 1962 ($6). (See pages 191-214.)

Ronald M. Schneider, *Communism in Guatemala, 1944-1954,* New York, Praeger, 1958. (See pages 5-14.)

26. South Africa

Mary Benson, *The African Patriots: The Story of the African National Congress of South Africa,* 310 pp., London, Faber, and Chicago, Encyclopedia Britannica Press, 1964 ($5.95). Paperback title: *South Africa: The Struggle for a Birth Right,* New York, Funk & Wagnalls, 1966 ($2.50).

_____, *Chief Albert Lutuli of South Africa,* London, Oxford University Press, 1963.

Edward Feit, *African Opposition in South Africa: The Failure of Passive Resistance,* 223 pp., Stanford, Cal., Hoover Institution on War, Revolution and Peace, 1967. (Campaigns of 1954-55.)

Leo Kuper, *Passive Resistance in South Africa,* 256 pp., New Haven, Yale University Press, 1957, and London, Jonathan Cape, 1956. (The 1952 Defiance Campaign.)

Albert Luthuli, *Let My People Go,* New York, McGraw-Hill and London, Collins, 1962. Paperback edition: New York, Meridian, World, 1969 ($2.65).

Edward Roux, *Time Longer than Rope: A History of the Black Man's Struggle for Freedom in South Africa* (second edition), 469 pp., Madison, Wisc. University of Wisconsin Press, 1964 (text edition $6.50, paperback $2.95).

Gene Sharp, "Can Nonviolence Work in South Africa? . . .", *Peace News,* London, June 21, June 28, July 5, and October 25, 1963.

See also other items listed in Nonviolent Action: A Selected Bibliography.

27. East Germany, 1953

Heinz Brandt, "The East German Popular Uprising," in *The Review*, No. 2, October, 1969, Brussels, Imry Nagy Institute for Political Research.

Stefan Brant, *The East German Rising*, New York, Praeger, 1957, and London, Thames & Hudson, 1955.

Rainer Hildebrandt, *The Explosion: The Uprising Behind the Iron Curtain*, 198 pp., Boston, Little Brown, 1955.

Theodor Ebert, "Nonviolent Resistance Against Communist Regimes?", in Roberts (ed), *Civilian Resistance as a National Defense (op. cit.)*.

William Robert Miller, *Nonviolence: A Christian Interpretation (op. cit.)*, pp. 249-256.

28. Soviet Prison Camps, esp. 1953

Paul Barton, "The Strike Mechanism in Soviet Concentration Camps," in *Monthly Information Bulletin*, No. 4 (August-November, 1955) of the International Commission Against Concentration Camp Practices, pp. 19-27. (In this issue, see also pp. 28-35: "The Ninety-Six Day Strike in the Norilsk Camps," and pp. 66-68: "Concentration Camp Questions in International Publications.")

————, "The Transformation of the Soviet Concentrationary System," in *Saturn Monthly Review* (new title of *Monthly Information Bulletin*), Vol. II, No. 1 (January-February, 1956), pp. 32-45.

————, "Have the Soviet Camps Taken a New Turn?" in *Saturn Monthly Review*, Vol. II, No. 2 (March-May, 1956), pp. 16-20. (See also Vol. II, No. 5 (December, 1956), pp. 123-124: "Concentration Camp Questions in International Publications.")

Brigitte Gerland, "How the Great Vorkuta Strike Was Prepared," and "The Great Labor Camp Strike at Vorkuta," in *The Militant* (New York), February 28 and March 7, 1955.

153

Joseph Scholmer, *Vorkuta,* New York, Holt, Rinehart & Winston, 1955, and London, Weidenfeld and Nicolson, 1954. (Excerpt in Sibley (ed), *The Quiet Battle.)*

29. Hungary, 1956

Tamas Aczel (ed), *Ten Years After: The Revolution in the Perspective of History,* 253 pp., New York *et al.,* Holt, Rinehart, & Winston, 1967, and London, MacGibbon & Kee, 1966. (See especially the appendices by Stephen Barley, "Bibliography of the Hungarian Revolution" and "Hungary – a Chronology of Events, 1953-65.")

Melvin J. Lasky, *The Hungarian Revolution: A White Book, The Story of the October Uprising as Recorded in Documents, Dispatches, Eye-Witness Accounts, and World-Wide Reactions,* 318 pp., London, Martin Secker & Warbug, 1957, for the Congress of Cultural Freedom.

Tibor Meray, *Thirteen Days That Shook the Kremlin: Imre Nagy and the Hungarian Revolution,* 290 pp., London, Thames & Hudson, 1959.

George Mikes, *The Hungarian Revolution,* 148 pp., London, André Deutsch, 1957.

Report of the Special Committee on the Problem of Hungary, General Assembly, Official Records: Eleventh Session, Supplement No. 18 (A/3592), New York, United Nations, 1957.

Ferenc A. Vali, *Rift and Revolt in Hungary: Nationalism versus Communism,* Cambridge, Mass., Harvard University Press, and London, Oxford Press, 1961.

Paul E. Zinner, *Revolution in Hungary,* 380 pp., New York and London, Columbia University Press, 1962. (See especially the third part and the bibliographical note.)
See also bibliographies in William Griffith, "The Revolt Reconsidered" in East Europe, *(NYC) Vol. 9, No. 7 (July 1960) and other items cited in* Nonviolent Action: A Selected Bibliography.

30. U. S. Civil Rights

Herbert Garfinkel, *When Negroes March: The March on Washington Movement in the Organizational Politics for FEPC,* 224 pp., New York, Atheneum, 1969, (paperback $2.95).

Tom Kahn, *Unfinished Revolution,* 64 pp., New York, Igal Rodenko, 1960. (The sit-in movement of 1960.)

Martin Luther King, Jr., *Stride Toward Freedom,* 230 pp., New York, Harper & Row, 1968 (hardcover $4.95, paperback $ .75). (Primarily about the Montgomery bus boycott, and the moral basis of nonviolence.)

_____, *Why We Can't Wait,* 159 pp., New York, Harper & Row, 1964 (hardcover $4.95, paperback $ .60). New York, Signet New American Library, 1964.

Anthony Lewis and The New York Times, *The Second American Revolution: A First Hand Account of the Struggle for Civil Rights,* 271 pp., New York, Random House, 1964 (hardcover $7.95), and London, Hamish Hamilton, 1963.

Louis E. Lomax, *The Negro Revolt,* 271 pp., New York, Harper & Row, 1962 (hardcover $6.50), New York, Signet New American Library, 1963 (paperback $ .95). London, Hamish Hamilton, 1963.

_____, *To Kill A Black Man,* Los Angeles, Holloway House Publishing Co., 1968 (paperback $ .95). (See chapters 8 and 15.)

James Peck, *Cracking the Color Line: Non-violent Direct Action Methods of Eliminating Racial Discrimination,* 32 pp. pamphlet, New York, Congress of Racial Equality, 1961.

_____, *Freedom Ride,* 125 pp., New York, Grove Press, 1962.

Merrill Proudfoot, *Diary of a Sit-in,* 204 pp., Chapel Hill, N.C., University of North Carolina Press, 1962 (hardcover $5). New Haven, Conn., College and University Press (paperback $1.95).

Arthur I. Waskow, *From Race Riot to Sit-In, 1919 and the* 155

1960's, 380 pp., Chapters XII-XVII, New York, Doubleday, 1966 (paperback $1.95).

Alan F. Westin (ed), *Freedom Now! The Civil-Rights Struggle In America,* 346 pp. (Parts II and IV) New York, Basic Books, 1964 ($6.95).

Howard Zinn, *SNCC: The New Abolitionists,* 286 pp., Boston, Beacon Press, 1965 (text edition $4.95, paperback $1.95).

See also the bibliography in Westin's Freedom Now! *and Elizabeth Miller, compiler,* The Negro in America: A Bibliography, *190 pp., Cambridge, Mass., Harvard University Press, 1966. (See pp. 140-154.)*

31. M. L. King, Jr.: Biographies

Lerone Bennett, Jr., *What Manner of Man: Martin Luther King, Jr.,* Chicago, Johnson Publishing Co., Inc., 1968. See pp. 37-39, 69-72, 74-77.

David L. Lewis, *King: A Critical Biography,* 472 pp., New York, Praeger, 1970.

William Robert Miller, *Martin Luther King,* New York, Weybright & Talley, Inc., 1968. (See chapter 4.)

L. D. Reddick, *Crusador Without Violence: A Biography of Martin Luther King,* 243 pp., New York, Harper and Bros., 1959.

32. Danilo Dolci: Biographies

James McNeish, *Fire Under the Ashes: The Life of Danilo Dolci,* 256 pp., Boston, Beacon Press, 1966 ($5.95), and London, Hodder and Staughton, 1965.

Melville Harcourt, *Portraits of Destiny,* New York, Sheed and Ward, 1966. (See pp. 49-97.)

Jerre Mangione, *A Passion for Sicilians: The World Around Danilo Dolci,* 369 pp., New York, William Morrow & Co., 1968.

33. South Vietnam, 1963

David Halberstam, *The Making of a Quagmire,* 323 pp.,

New York, Random House, 1965 (hardcover $5.95), and London, The Bodley Head, 1965. (Especially pp. 194-243.)

Jean Lacouture, *Vietnam: Between Two Truces*, 295 pp., New York, Random House, 1966 (paperback $1.95).

Adam Roberts, "Buddhism and Politics in South Vietnam," in *The World Today* (London), June 1964, and "The Buddhists, the War, and the Vietcong," in *ibid.*, May 1966.

See other references in Nonviolent Action: A Selected Bibliography.

34. Cesar Chavez and the Grape Strike

John Gregory Dunne, *Delano: The Story of the California Grape Strike*, 176 pp., New York, Farrar, Straus & Giroux, 1967 (paperback $1.95).

Peter Matthiessen, *Sal Si Puedes: Cesar Chavez and the New American Revolution*, 372 pp., New York, Random House, 1969 ($6.95).

Stan Steiner, *La Raza: The Mexican Americans*, 418 pp., New York, Evanston, and London, Harper & Row, 1970 ($8.95). (Especially pp. 310-323 on Cesar Chavez.)

35. Czechoslovakia — 1968

Robert Littell (ed), *The Czech Black Book*, 303 pp., New York, Praeger, 1969 (hardcover $6.95), and New York, Avon (paperback $1.25).

Harvy Schwartz, *Prague's 200 Days: The Struggle for Democracy in Czechoslovakia*, 274 pp., New York, Praeger, 1969 ($5.95). (Primarily on democratization before the invasion.)

Robin Alison Remington (ed), *Winter in Prague*, 473 pp., Cambridge, Mass., MIT Press, 1970 (hardcover $12.50, paperback $2.95).

Joseph Wechsberg, *The Voices*, Garden City, N. Y., Doubleday, 1969.

Philip Windsor and Adam Roberts, *Czechoslovakia 1968: Reform, Repression and Resistance,* 200 pp., New York, Columbia University Press, 1969, and London, Chatto & Windus, 1969 (hardcover $7.50, paperback, $2.50).

A larger multilithed bibliography on Czechoslovakia edited by Carl Horne is available in limited numbers from Dr. Gene Sharp, Defense Without War Seminar, Harvard University, Center for International Affairs, 6 Divinity Ave., Cambridge, Mass. 02138.

Other Cases:

For bibliographies on other cases, see listing in *Nonviolent Action: A Selected Bibliography* (including Central Africa, Gold Coast, resistance to the 1961 French Generals' Revolt, woman suffrage movements, Belgian general strike of 1913 and various others. See also Miller, *Nonviolence,* and Sharp, *The Politics of Nonviolent Action.*

PACIFISM

37. Principled Nonviolence

This is a separate phenomenon from nonviolent action, which sometimes is, and more often is not, related to it. On the types of principled nonviolence see:

Peter Mayer (ed), *The Pacifist Conscience,* 447 pp., New York, Holt, Rinehart & Winston, 1966 and London, Rupert Hart-Davis, 1966.

Gene Sharp, "Types of Principled Nonviolence," in A. Paul Hare and Herbert H. Blumberg (eds), *Nonviolent Direct Action: American Cases: Social-Psychological Analyses,* pp. 273-313, Washington, D.C., Corpus Books, 1969 ($10).

On further bibliography, see footnotes to that chapter, and the recommended bibliographies, Nonviolent Action *and* To End War, *and also Miller (ed),* Bibliography of Books on War, Pacifism, Nonviolence and Related Studies *(Nyack, New York, Fellowship of Reconciliation, 1960). See also discussion and references on principled nonviolence from various of the anthologies and general studies of the 1920's and 1930's.*

38. Conscientious objection and war resistance

Bibliographies of these subjects are available in the following sources:

A. Carter, D. Hoggett, A. Roberts (eds), *Nonviolent Action: A Selected Bibliography,* pp. 36-38, 39-40.

R. Pickus and R. Woito, *To End War,* pp. 117-121.

William Robert Miller (ed), *Bibliography of Books on War Pacifism, Nonviolence and Related Studies,* pp. 22-23.

A NOTE TO YOU:

If in your research you discover or develop a new bibliography for cases which are not included here at all, or if you find important sources which should be added to these listings in a future revision, would you be good enough to send along a copy? Your discoveries might help others. Send to Dr. Gene Sharp, Harvard University, Center for International Affairs, 6 Divinity Avenue, Cambridge, Massachusetts, 02138.

ACKNOWLEDGEMENTS

"Creative Conflict in Politics" originally appeared in *New Era,* January, 1962, and was reprinted as a pamphlet by Housmans, London, 1962. It appears here in somewhat revised form, with changes and additions in the case studies.

"National Defense Without Armaments: A Radical Approach to Peace and Security," originally appeared in *War/Peace Report,* New York, April, 1970, pp. 3-10.

"The Technique of Nonviolent Action" appeared originally in *The Strategy of Civilian Defence: Nonviolent Resistance to Aggression,* edited by Adam Roberts, London, Faber and Faber, 1967. The American edition of this work was published in 1968 by Stackpole Books, Harrisburg, Pennsylvania, under the title: *Civilian Resistance as a National Defense: Nonviolent Action Against Agression.*

Chapter 4 is a revision of a paper, "Research Areas on the Nature, Problems, and Potentialities of Civilian Defense," presented *in absentia* at a Seminar held by the Indian Institute of Advanced Study in Simla, India, on "Gandhi: Theory and Practice, Social Impact and Contemporary Relevance," October 13-26, 1968, and published in its proceedings in 1969. Jessie Jones has assisted most valuably in the revision, editing, and restructuring of this chapter. Numerous research problems and topics have been incorporated in this chapter from suggestions made by a large number of individuals in articles, memoranda, correspondence, and conversations. Acknowledgement is especially due to the Hon. Alastair Buchan, April Carter, Theodor Ebert, Irving Janis, Jessie Jones, Daniel Katz, Herbert Kelman, Sandi Mandeville, Ronald McCarthy, Charles Nathan, Robert Nozick, the late Lars Porsholt, Adam Roberts, Theodor Roszak, Kenneth Wadoski, and Kurt H. Wolff. Apologies to any who have unintentionally not been listed.

The 85 Cases of Nonviolent Action is an expanded version of material originally appearing in Adam Roberts, Jerome Frank, Arne Naess and Gene Sharp, *Civilian Defence* (pamphlet), London, Peace News, 1964.

The Course Program in Civilian Defense was prepared for this book by William B. Watson.

For their aid in the compilation of Selected Further Readings, the author gratefully acknowledges the assistance of Margaret Jane Brady, Dennis Brady, and Ken Currier.

The Author:

Dr. Gene Sharp is presently a research fellow at Harvard University's Center for International Affairs, visiting lecturer at Brandeis University, and Associate Professor of Sociology and Political Science at Southeastern Massachusetts Institute of Technology. He received his B.A. and M.A. in sociology from Ohio State University, and Doctor of Philosophy from Oxford University, where he is a life member of St. Catherine's College. Dr. Sharp was assistant editor of the weekly *Peace News* in London for three years; he did research in nonviolent action at the Institute for Social Research in Oslo, Norway; was assistant lecturer at the Institute of Philosophy and the History of Ideas at the University of Oslo; and from 1965 to 1970 was a member of the Harvard-MIT joint Arms Control Seminar. He has taught courses in his field of research at Harvard University, Boston University, Lesley College, the University of Massachusetts at Boston, and at the Experimental College of Tufts University. Dr. Sharp is the author of many books and articles on the subjects of nonviolent action and civilian defense. His major work, *The Politics of Nonviolent Action,* is scheduled for publication by Pilgrim Press in 1971.

The Course Program in Civilian Defense was prepared for this book by William B. Watson.

Cover Design by Raymond Parks

An Extending Horizons Book
Porter Sargent Publisher
11 Beacon Street, Boston, Mass. 02108